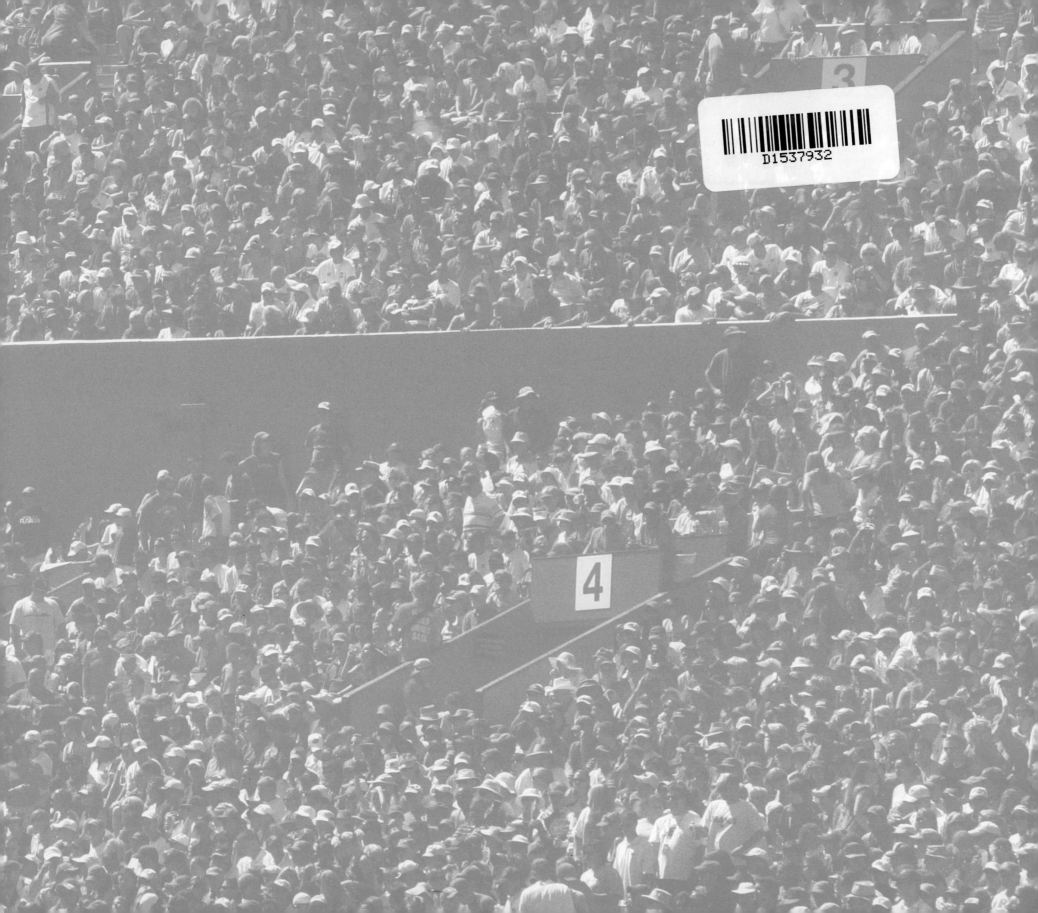

FLORIDA FOOTBALL
YESTERDAY & TODAY™

PAT DOOLEY

FOREWORD BY JACK YOUNGBLOOD

WEST
SIDE
PUBLISHING

Pat Dooley is an award-winning sports columnist for *The Gainesville Sun*, where he has been covering the Gators for more than 20 years. He is a regular on radio shows in Gainesville and Jacksonville, as well as other sports talk shows around the country. Dooley's work has also appeared in numerous magazines.

Jack Youngblood came to the University of Florida as a skinny project and left as an All-American. He starred for the Gators from 1968 to 1970 and is one of five players in the school's Ring of Honor. During his NFL career, Youngblood made seven Pro Bowls and was twice NFC Defensive Player of the Year. He is best known for playing in Super Bowl XIV with a broken leg. In 2001, Youngblood became the first Gator to be named to the Pro Football Hall of Fame.

Factual verification by Nathan Rush.

Special thanks to Ron Mobley for the use of his memorabilia collection. Mobley earned his undergraduate and graduate degrees from Florida and has been a lifelong Gator fan. His collection reflects not only Gator Nation pride but a family history of attendance at UF over several generations.

We would also like to thank Joyce Dewsbury and Laurie N. Taylor from the University of Florida Archives.

Page 73: *The Panama City News Herald* clip reprinted with permission from *The News Herald*, © 1967.

Yesterday & Today is a trademark of Publications International, Ltd.

West Side Publishing is a division of Publications International, Ltd.

Louis Weber, CEO
Publications International, Ltd.
7373 North Cicero Avenue
Lincolnwood, Illinois 60712

Permission is never granted for commercial purposes.

ISBN-13: 978-1-4127-6111-6
ISBN-10: 1-4127-6111-5

Manufactured in China.

8 7 6 5 4 3 2 1

Library of Congress Control Number: 2009923893

Pictured on the front cover: Tim Tebow
Pictured on the back cover: 2007 Florida Gators

Picture Credits:

Front cover: ***Sports Illustrated*/Getty Images**

Back cover: **Getty Images**

Dave Akins: 39 (bottom); **Courtesy Alachua County Historic Trust, Matherson Museum, Inc.:** 48 (top right), 49 (top left); **Alamy Images:** Patrick Lynch, 3; **AP Images:** 6, 47 (left), 51, 65 (left), 66 (left), 79, 109 (bottom); **© Corbis:** David Bergman, 129 (left); Bettmann, 64, 67 (top), 69 (right); **Doug Tonks Collection:** 135 (bottom); **Courtesy FLAJAX.COM:** 19 (top right); **Georgia Sports Hall of Fame:** 61 (bottom left); **Getty Images:** endsheets, 11 (right), 75, 89, 92 (bottom), 93, 96 (left), 97, 101, 102 (right), 104, 105, 106, 107, 108, 109 (top), 112 (bottom), 114 (bottom), 115, 116, 117, 118, 119, 120, 121, 122, 123, 126, 127 (bottom), 129 (right), 130 (left), 131, 132 (bottom), 133 (left), 140, 141; AFP, 113 (bottom); Collegiate Images, 7, 42 (right), 82, 84 (bottom), 94 (left), 96 (right); *Sports Illustrated*, 36, 59 (bottom), 71, 78, 80, 83 (bottom), 90 (bottom), 91 (top), 92 (top), 95, 100, 102 (left), 103, 112 (top), 113 (top), 128 (top), 130 (right), 133 (right), 137, 138; **The Panama City News Herald:** 73 (top right); **PIL Collection:** 18 (top left & bottom), 19 (top left), 32 (top left & bottom), 33 (top left & bottom), 48 (bottom right), 60, 61 (top left & top right), 72 (top left & top center), 73 (bottom left & bottom center), 86, 87 (top right & top center), 98 (top right, bottom left & bottom right), 99, 110 (bottom left & bottom right), 111 (top center, top right & bottom center), 114 (top), 124, 125 (top left, left center & right), 127 (top), 134 (top left, top center, top right & bottom right), 135 (top left & top right), 142; **Ron Mobley Collection:** 18 (top right), 38, 49 (bottom), 61 (bottom right), 69 (left), 70, 72 (top right & bottom), 73 (top left & bottom right), 87 (top left, bottom left & bottom right), 98 (top left), 110 (top left & top right), 111 (top left & bottom left), 125 (bottom), 134 (bottom left), 135 (top center); **University of Florida Archives:** 8, 9, 10, 11 (left), 12, 13, 14, 15, 16, 17, 19 (bottom), 20, 21, 22, 23, 24, 25, 26, 27, 28, 29, 30, 31, 32 (top right), 33, 34, 35, 37, 39 (top), 40, 41, 43, 44, 45, 46, 47 (right), 48 (left), 49 (top right), 50, 52, 53, 54, 55, 56, 57, 58, 59 (top), 60, 62, 63, 65 (right), 67 (bottom), 68, 74, 76, 77, 81, 83 (top), 84 (top), 85, 88, 90 (top), 91 (bottom); Department of Special Collections, George A. Smathers Libraries, 42 (left); Special Collections, 66 (right); **WireImage:** 94 (right), 128 (bottom); **www.gatorzone.com:** 132 (top)

Memorabilia photography: **PDR Productions, Inc./Peter Rossi**

The home of the Florida Gators was built in 1930 and renamed Ben Hill Griffin Stadium in 1989. But most UF fans lovingly refer to it as "The Swamp."

CONTENTS

UF's early teams   *p. 13*

Gator memorabilia   *p. 32*

The birth of the SEC   *p. 36*

Game Day   p. 55

Albert the Alligator   p. 91

Steve Spurrier   p. 102

Foreword

My journey with the University of Florida began in the fall of 1966 on my high school football field. My team, the Jefferson County Tigers, had just won Florida's state championship when Gator baseball head coach Dave Fuller approached me and said these life-altering words: "Son, how would you like to be a Florida Gator?"

Considering a scout had previously told me that I would never play college football, I couldn't quite comprehend what was happening, especially at the age of 17. I had certainly heard and read about the Florida Gators,

Jack Youngblood's years at Florida were just the beginning. He would go on to have an illustrious NFL career and receive various football honors.

but I never dreamed that I, a country boy from Monticello, Florida, could be a part of that world. I think I was still dreaming when in August 1967 my mother dropped me off at the curb in Gainesville, with my sole possessions in one suitcase, in front of the magnificent stadium that would be my home for the next four years.

My first challenge was to make the football team . . . and to save my hair! The upperclassmen held a meeting the week before the freshman team was to play Florida State's freshmen in Tallahassee. The older boys convinced us underclassmen that they would shave our heads if we lost to FSU. To our good fortune, we came home with a big "W" and a huge sigh of relief!

As a sophomore, I was the kicker in my varsity debut, and my first kickoff was returned for a touchdown by a speedy Air Force player. Fortunately, I was able to redeem myself during that game by kicking a 42-yard field goal that provided the margin needed for victory.

I also have fond memories of the tremendous 1969 season. We began that season by playing the Houston Cougars at Florida Field. Houston was ranked No. 1 in the national polls, and that team had been using a new, innovative offense in college football: the Houston Veer. We knew it was our job to stop that offense. I don't know if we necessarily succeeded at that, but we did come away with a 59–34 win.

A couple of weeks later we beat FSU 21–6 before a then-record crowd. Our defensive line dropped FSU quarterback Bill Cappleman 11 times, and three Seminole players ended up with minus 18 yards rushing. I remember sacking Cappleman four or five times and recovering two of his fumbles in what coach Ray Graves called "the best pass rush we've

Youngblood was one of Florida's all-time best defensive backs, suiting up for the Gators from 1968 to '70.

ever had here"—a real compliment since it was always nice to please the coach. We ended the 1969 season with a 9–1–1 record, which was the best in the school's history at the time, and a 14–13 victory over the Tennessee Volunteers in the Gator Bowl.

As a senior, a highlight that stands out is when I caused and recovered a fumble to stop a University of Georgia Bulldog drive. That same game saw John Reaves throw a couple of touchdown passes to Carlos Alvarez (which seemed to happen on a weekly basis while I was in Gainesville) to win that year's "World's Largest Outdoor Cocktail Party."

Being a Gator, competing in the SEC, playing in a bowl game, making All-America teams—these are all memories that I cherish. But none can compare to the lifelong, profound relationships I made on and off the field during my years at the University of Florida. Robert Harrell, my

right defensive end, is my "brother from another mother"—so much more than just another guy on the football team. Ray Pilcher and Tommy Durrance are also like family, not just guys in the locker room. The bonds created during the challenges and successes on the football field have only strengthened as we each took different roads in life, facing ups and downs along the way.

But this is just my story. With *Florida Football: Yesterday & Today*™, you can relive the many great moments and players of the game and catch a glimpse of the extraordinary experiences of "the boys from ol' Florida." All Gators are proud of the faithful tradition that surrounds the football program, and to be a small part of the success of that tradition is in itself rewarding. To this day we eat, sleep, and bleed Orange and Blue. From the south to the north, east to west, our hearts swell and our eyes smile when we hear "Go Gators!"

Jack Youngblood

> "Being a Gator, competing in the SEC, playing in a bowl game, making All-America teams—these are all memories that I cherish."
>
> **Jack Youngblood**

HUMBLE BEGINNINGS

1906–1919

In the beginning, there was no Gator Nation. The evolution of
Florida football to today's high-powered program started humbly.
But without this early history, the present wouldn't be the same.
Before the Internet and recruiting rankings, before helmets and
wristbands, before Gatorade and Gator glory, there were a handful
of lads in leggings who played for the love of the game.

It was a rudimentary beginning for Florida football, the 1903 team declaring itself "champions" with just a one-game schedule. But every school, every program, has to start somewhere.

Early Florida football was hardly the scrutinized and idolized program it would become over a 100-plus year history. But the players still fought for every yard and first down.

Before They Were Gators

When Florida started playing football, it wasn't the Gators. It wasn't the orange and blue. It wasn't in Gainesville. And it wasn't even the University of Florida.

But any historical reference to the beginning of Florida football must include the state's very first team—the 1899 Florida Agricultural College team. FAC was located in Lake City, Florida, 35 miles north of Gainesville. The team went unbeaten because it couldn't find anybody to play.

It would be two years before FAC players would put toe to leather, and two more years before the school would change its name to the University of Florida. The pre-UF boys, wearing blue and white, showed up late to the Jacksonville Fairgrounds on November 22, 1901, where a stump on the field interfered with play in a 6–0 loss to Stetson, believed to be the first intercollegiate game ever played in the state.

The FAC was renamed the University of Florida in 1903, and the team beat East Florida Seminary, located in Gainesville, in its only game that year. By 1904, Florida had a University Athletic Association and boosters. Soon, it would have a new home.

In 1905, Gainesville and Lake City squared off in a battle to see which city would be home to UF. The state

Many of Florida's early games were played in either Jacksonville or Gainesville against the Jacksonville Riverside Athletic Club. The two teams played two games a season during the first three years of Florida's fledgling program.

legislature had recently passed the Buckman Act, which consolidated all state-supported schools into one college for white males, one for white females, and one for African Americans. Both towns offered $40,000 and land for the new men's college. Gainesville won the vote 6–4, and the University of Florida would one day be synonymous with the city.

The real beginning of the Florida football team is marked by the hiring of J. A. "Pee Wee" Forsythe as its first official coach in 1906. He was a star player for the team at the time and a talent in great demand. In fact, he left the team to become the coach at semi-pro Jacksonville Riverside during UF's first season. He returned to coach two more years and left an indelible mark on the program as "the father of Florida football."

Forsythe, who came to Gainesville from a stint in Tallahassee as the coach at Florida State College, coached Florida in its first-ever home game in 1906, a 6–0 win over Rollins College in the city's baseball park near Gainesville's current downtown area. Admission was 50 cents, and an estimated 150 fans watched as Forsythe's Minnesota Shift offense, which started with the two guards and center at the line of scrimmage and everybody else in the backfield until they shifted into position, finally got rolling in the second half. The winning score came from halfback Roy Corbett, who would be captain of the 1907 team.

Florida's record books actually list a pair of games played in 1906 prior to the Rollins game—Gainesville AC (presumably Athletic Club) and Mercer—that are now considered unofficial.

Forsythe's game to remember came in Savannah in 1907. Savannah Agricultural College's football team, a collection of former college semi-pro players, had smashed Florida 27–2 in Forsythe's first season. During the rematch in Savannah, his touchdown sparked UF to a 6–0 win in front of a crowd of 600. The Savannah fans had not seen their team lose at home in six years, and the news of the win brought about a wild celebration back in Gainesville. The Florida–Georgia rivalry was born.

That Florida team also won the state championship, but all that meant in 1907 was that the Florida boys had beaten Rollins and Jacksonville AC, in addition to Savannah AC.

Members of UF's 1907 team pose for a photo. The team got revenge on the Savannah AC team that had beaten them 27–2 the year before with a 6–0 win in Georgia.

The Orange and Blue

In the history of college football, some nicknames have come from contests. School colors are often carefully chosen. In the case of Florida, it was all a bit of a fluke.

The story of why the University of Florida teams fly under an orange and blue flag and answer to the name "Gators" first appeared in a newspaper piece from the August 19, 1948, edition of the *Florida Times-Union*. The story goes that Phillip Miller, owner of the popular off-campus drugstore Miller's in Gainesville, decided the fledgling football team was popular enough that students would purchase pennants.

During a visit in 1907 to see his son Austin at the University of Virginia in Charlottesville, the two visited the Michie Company, which manufactured pennants and banners. They were shown samples from schools like Princeton and Yale—schools that had nicknames. Florida did not. Austin Miller allegedly blurted out, "Alligators," and a tradition was born.

Once the pennants began to appear in Miller's in 1908, Southerners quickly shortened the nickname to Gators. And when the pennants arrived, they were blue with orange alligators on them. Just like that, Florida had school colors that would one day turn into the "Orange-Blue" cheer that rocks the stadium today.

While the orange and blue color combination of the Florida Gators was a bit of a fluke, it sure stands out against the green football turf of any field in college football.

Pyle Driver

When G. E. Pyle took over the reins of the Florida team in 1909, he put together an impressive record of 26–7–3. But those first years of playing the two state schools—Stetson and Rollins—and club teams from other cities didn't sit well with the new coach. He had inherited a strong team from Forsythe and wanted to see how the Gators would stand up against established out-of-state teams.

Pyle pushed Florida into the Southern Intercollegiate Athletic Association and scheduled the likes of Clemson, South Carolina, Georgia Tech, and Auburn. Pyle, who played running back his first two years at UF, also turned the football program into a money-making opportunity by reorganizing the athletic association.

It was under Pyle that the Gators recorded a landmark victory, beating South Carolina 10–6 at home on October 19, 1912, when Hoyle Pounds fell on a Carolina fumble in the end zone as the Gamecocks tried to return a short dropkick attempt by Earle "Dummy" Taylor. It was Florida's first victory over a major out-of-state opponent.

The tougher schedule meant more losses for Pyle's teams and also led to a motto that became infamous in Gator lore during the 1960s: "Wait 'Til Next Year." The lament came from an editorial in UF's student newspaper,

Florida began moving away from playing club teams and started playing more college teams under G. E. Pyle. That included the first game against South Carolina, a 6–6 tie, in 1911.

The Alligator. After a combined five losses in 1912 and 1913, Pyle resigned in the spring of 1914.

Historic Hammering

Three years before Georgia Tech's football team set an unbreakable record with a 222–0 win over Cumberland, G. E. Pyle's final team at Florida put up a score that was almost as overwhelming. On October 6, 1913, Florida beat Florida Southern College 144–0.

And it could have been worse. Florida scored 22 touchdowns—seven of them by Harvey Hester—and had another called back because of a holding penalty. Florida Southern, located in Lakeland, did not record a first down in the game, which was played according to high school rules with 12-minute quarters.

Team captain Louis Tenny was the story early in the game, throwing for UF's first two scores and running it in from 15 yards for a third. He finished the game with five rushing touchdowns, while George Mosely added three. Tubby Price kicked 12 extra points but missed the other 10.

The mighty Gators were brought down to earth the following week, losing 55–0 to Auburn.

G. E. Pyle was Florida's second head football coach and lasted five seasons. He never had a losing record, and his first three teams went an impressive 17–2–2, including an unbeaten mark in 1911.

Close, but No Cigar

Although it would be 40 years until the Gators would play in a sanctioned bowl game on American soil, coach G. E. Pyle did take his team on a bowl trip of sorts after the 1912 regular season. The Gators were scheduled to play Louisiana State University, but a conference ruling that all games must be played before Thanksgiving Day cancelled that matchup.

Instead, an invitation came for two games to be played in Cuba, with the first to be held on Christmas Day. After playing against a club team in Tampa, Florida, and winning easily 44–0 in a practice game, the Gators set sail for the capital of Cuba, Havana. There, they were treated royally. During their stay, the Florida players enjoyed some down time, one day boarding a yacht for a leisurely excursion and also attending a party at the Vedado Athletic Club.

Florida's 1912 team took a trip to Cuba and hammered the Vedado Club of Havana 28–0.

The team had plenty of fun until Cuban police intervened in the second "bowl" game after coach G. E. Pyle pulled his players from the field.

When it came time for the games to be played, the Florida Gators handled the Vedado Athletic Club team 28–0 in the first game. As for the second game five days later, there is no record in the Florida media guide. In Cuba, it's in the record books as a 1–0 forfeit victory for the Cuban club.

A crowd of around 1,500 showed up to see the second "bowl" game. Upset that the Cuban team was employing the flying wedge, a dangerous formation of colliding bodies outlawed in the United States, coach Pyle pulled his team off the field after arguing intently with the official, who was a former coach of the Cuban team. There was no shortage of cops who were paying customers at the game, so Pyle was arrested, taken to jail, and released for trial the next day. Pyle and his team bolted for the ship *Olivette* and sailed home safely about an hour before the trial was to take place.

Early Heroes

In the formative years of Florida football, there was no shortage of stars on the gridiron for the Gators. Probably the best of them all was a kid from Gainesville—Earle "Dummy" Taylor. It's not clear why he was referred to by such an insulting nickname, but he did need five years to graduate. He was also the king of the hidden ball trick.

In those five seasons, Taylor was a versatile player who kicked three field goals in an 11–0 win over the Olympic Club of Jacksonville in 1909 and ran for touchdowns covering 45, 60, and 75 yards against Rollins the same year. His field goal records stood until the mid-1970s, and he is the only Gator player to earn five letters.

Earle "Dummy" Taylor, the master of the hidden ball trick and an adept dropkicker, could do it all for Florida. Taylor was a Gainesville native who ran for three long touchdowns in a 1909 game against Rollins.

The Alligator, UF's student newspaper, perhaps summed it up best: "To Dummy must go the credit more than any one man of putting Florida on the football map."

The Shands brothers also played major roles in Florida's early success. W. A. "Bill" Shands, also a Gainesville kid, was a quarterback, a center, and an end who went on to a career in the state legislature. The school's teaching hospital is named after him. His brother Jim was also part of a dangerous backfield along with Taylor in 1908 and scored the winning touchdown in a big win over Rollins the previous season. William "Gric" Gibbs was the captain of the 1908 team and a starting fullback and tackle. He played a game in a win over Rollins in 1907 despite being ill with what turned out to be malaria.

Florida standout W. A. Shands would later find success off the field as well, when he was elected to the Florida state legislature.

> **"To Dummy must go the credit more than any one man of putting Florida on the football map."**
>
> *The Alligator*

McCoy: Three Years and Out

Florida football was gaining popularity by the 1915 season. For this game against Sewanee, fans who couldn't get close to the action figured out that the best way to see a game was to stand on the seats of their cars.

Two of Florida's three biggest rivalry games each season are Tennessee and Georgia (Florida State being the other). Fans have Charles J. McCoy to thank for that. McCoy, who took over as coach after G. E. Pyle moved on, had immediate success. His 1914 team won five of seven games, including the last four, and outscored opponents 152–46.

A former coach at Sewanee Military Academy, McCoy added Georgia to the Gators' schedule the following year and Tennessee the year after that. The first Florida–Georgia game in 1915 was played, fittingly enough, in Jacksonville (the series would move there on a permanent basis in 1933). But McCoy bit off more than he could chew that first game. The Bulldogs rolled to a 37–0 victory, and the Gators finished the season 4–3.

It would get worse in McCoy's final season as the Florida coach. With an ambitious schedule that included

Charles McCoy lasted only three seasons at Florida with a 9–10 record, including a 0–5 final season. But he did start the rivalries with Georgia and Tennessee, adding both to UF's schedule.

not only Georgia and Tennessee but also Alabama and Auburn, Florida went 0–5 and failed to score a touchdown, managing its only points on a field goal in a 14–3 loss to Indiana in the season finale.

Some of it was bad luck. McCoy had lost his starting tackles, J. Ham Dowling to transfer and Everett Yon to the National Guard, and had to move captain Rex Farrior from center to fullback. No matter the reasons, McCoy was dismissed after the winless season.

Still Not There

A. L. Busser continued a trend of Florida coaches who lasted only three years at the school. Busser did win his final three games and finished with a record of 7–8, with only one game being played in 1918 because of the war.

Before it would get better for football at the University of Florida, it would get worse. A lot worse.

Florida president Dr. A. A. Murphree looked to Wisconsin to hire away A. L. Busser to revive a program that was in trouble after the 0–5 season of 1916. Although Busser's Gators won their first game 21–13 against South Carolina on October 13, 1917, in Gainesville, the team would lose four of its next five by abysmal scores. The 68–0 loss to Auburn would be a particularly deflating outcome and would stand for 25 years as Florida's worst loss ever. The season closed with a 52–0 loss to Kentucky in Lexington on November 29. Florida was outscored that season by 200 points (247–47).

After a one-game season during World War I in 1918 (see sidebar), the 1919 season showed promise, with veterans returning from the war. But the chemistry between players who had stayed behind and those who had fought in the war wasn't there. After the team started 2–1, losing 16–0 to Georgia in Tampa, the Gators faced Florida Southern a week later in St. Petersburg. So confident was Busser (remember the 144–0 beating of Southern just six years earlier?) that some of the starters were held out at the beginning of the game.

It was a bad move. Florida lost 7–0, the lone score coming when center Tootie Perry's snap went left when it was supposed to go right and turned into a defensive touchdown.

Although Florida closed with three straight wins, including a 64–0 thrashing of rival Stetson, Busser's 7–8 overall record meant Florida was again looking for a new coach.

1918: A Terrible Year

As the 1918 season approached, the last thing on anyone's mind was sports. The United States had entered World War I in April 1917, and many UF players headed overseas to fight "The War to End All Wars."

Coupled with an influenza pandemic that affected almost one-third of the American population, fielding a football team was not a high priority. A. L. Busser saw his players leave before and during the season but managed to put together a team of sorts. The Gators played one game on October 5 in Gainesville against Camp Johnson, losing 14–2.

This plaque, which still stands at Ben Hill Griffin Stadium, honors the Florida men who fought and died in World War I. Their names are sealed within the plaque.

Game Day: Old School

Fleming Field, which lies between University Avenue and the current stadium, is a focal point of Florida football games today. The Gator Walk, a tradition before games when the players make their way to the stadium, cuts right through the middle of parking for boosters and media members.

What would a football game be without a band? Florida had several in the early days, but it was the marching band that serenaded the football team.

But in the early days of Florida football, it was the site of some of the biggest wins and toughest losses for the Gators. Although Florida's first game ever was played at the city baseball park, the team began playing on the small campus later in the 1906 season.

There, fans who paid $.50 per game or $1 for a season ticket would line the sidelines—the men in starched collars and suits and the women in long dresses—battling the Florida heat for a look at the team. Some fans beat the crowds by standing on the seats of their automobiles for a better view.

By 1910, a small set of bleachers was erected on Fleming Field. A few years later, Florida had its own marching band. A *Gainesville Sun* story on Florida's first official game in 1906 says only that the game "was well attended," but the crowds soon grew until the sidelines were three deep for the length of the field.

Fans waved their orange-and-blue pennants and used bugles and cowbells to make noise. The football team also had a pep club: It was called the Bo Gator Club and was established in the team's second season. The first Chief Bo Gator was Neal Storter, a student who would go on to play center and be the captain of the 1911 team.

It was a little easier to get a ticket in 1915 to see Florida's football team play than it is now. UF won this game against Mercer 34–7 to complete a 4–3 season.

The region that houses the University of Florida has its share of swampy areas, including this Green Sink on the university's grounds, shown here on a postcard in 1917.

It wasn't a sanctioned bowl game, but Florida's first postseason play made national news in 1912 when the Gators refused to finish the second game and were detained by Cuban police.

AMERICANS LEAVE FOOTBALL GAME; ALMOST ARRESTED

By United Press.

HAVANA, Dec. 28.—Members of the university of Florida football team are being held here tonight by the authorities as witnesses in a case brought against the promoter of a game between the American team and the Cuban athletics.

The Florida team played under 1912 rules and when the Cuban organization insisted on playing today under last year's rules the Americans left the field in the second quarter. Under the Cuban law all of the players refusing to complete the game could have been arrested and only the action of the promoter in assuming the responsibility saved the visitors from more serious complications.

This Tiffany lamp reproduction, featuring UF's trademark Gator, would be at home perched on the table of a Florida fan during the early 1900s as well as today.

The Gator Nation has always loved to gobble up souvenir items like this one—a leather football that is similar to the first ones used in college football. The "Gators" script on the side adds to its value.

This 1907 postcard shows the impressive beginnings of the university. The city of Gainesville beat out Lake City as the home of Florida's new men's college.

These players made up Florida's third official team in 1908 and had a respectable 5–2–1 record. The only game played that year against a team from out of state was an opening loss at Mercer in Macon, Georgia.

DELIGHTFUL DECADE

1920–1932

When the 1920s began, Florida's football program had already
been through four coaches and some difficult times on the field.
But this would be an era of new highs and new stars. What started
as a campus with two buildings tripled in size during the decade,
and a stadium was built, thanks to private donations.
This was truly the beginning of good times for the Gators.

*Carlos Proctor (left) and
Red Bethea, who still holds
the record for the third-
highest rushing game in
UF history, stand on
St. Augustine Beach,
where Charles Bachman
sometimes took his team
to train. Proctor went on
to become one of Florida's
first golf coaches in
1941 and '42.*

In his first three seasons, Charles Bachman coached Florida to a 22–6–1 record. The Gators started the 1931 season with a win at NC State and a tie against the University of North Carolina. But this 33–12 loss at Syracuse was a portent of things to come. Bachman won only 4 of his final 17 games before leaving for Michigan State in 1933.

A Fast Start

Until 1930, Florida played on-campus home games at Fleming Field, which is located to the north of where Ben Hill Griffin Stadium is today and adjacent to University Avenue. Fleming Field is now used on game days as parking for Bull Gators (UF's top athletic donors) and the media.

In search of a new coach for the 1920 season, school president Dr. A. A. Murphree looked to the Midwest, where he found William G. Kline. Kline had been a former star halfback at Illinois and a coach at Nebraska while finishing up his law degree. He guided the Gators to a 6–3 record his first year, which included a 1–0 forfeit win over Rollins College and a pair of shutouts against Stetson in Gainesville. Just five days after the second win over the Hatters, the team traveled to Columbus, Georgia, for a game on November 25, 1920, and lost to Oglethorpe 21–0.

In 1921 Florida went to Tuscaloosa on November 12 and surprised Alabama 9–2, the first win ever over the Tide, as part of a 6–3–2 season. The Gators played an 11th game for the first time, losing on December 3 in a postseason game to North Carolina 14–10 in Jacksonville.

Florida ventured into "big boy" football a year later when it traveled to Boston to play Harvard. Students were

let out of school on Wednesday to march with the team to the railroad station. On the train there was a large banner that read, "Dixie Land to Yankee Land." The team stopped in Washington, D.C., to meet sitting president Warren G. Harding before suffering a 24–0 loss in front of 50,000 fans at Soldiers Field.

That 1922 team finished 7–2, and Kline finished his coaching career with a strong 19–8–2 record. More importantly, he had found an assistant in James Van Fleet, who would succeed him as head coach in 1923 when Kline left to pursue a law career. Kline also brought in a player from the University of Arkansas, R. D. "Ark" Newton, who would account for 11 scores during that final season.

As Florida football moved into the 1920s, the Gators became more aggressive with their schedule, including a game at Harvard. In fact, when Florida played its first 11-game schedule in 1921, only four of the games were played in Gainesville.

Van Fleet Makes a Major Difference

Under General James Van Fleet, Florida began playing a national schedule but still found time to play games at Fleming Field, the home of the Gators until November 1930.

James Van Fleet was an Army major who was sent to Gainesville to help with the ROTC program (the ROTC building at UF now carries his name). He later would command troops as a four-star general during the Korean War. Van Fleet spent time in Greece in the 1940s, where he was the executor of the Truman Doctrine. The military strategies he used there and in Korea, which included withdrawing the front line and then counterattacking, are still used as teaching tools during officer training at the Pentagon.

Van Fleet's brilliant mind was displayed both in the military and on the football field. Florida went 12–3–4 during his two seasons as coach against a national schedule that included Army (where Van Fleet had been a fullback on the undefeated 1914 team), Texas, and Georgia Tech.

The major took his Gator teams on the road for most of those big games, playing only six games in two seasons in Gainesville. Twice his teams played to 7–7 ties against Georgia Tech in Atlanta, and in 1924 lost a tough game at West Point 14–7 despite a 95-yard interception return by Ark Newton.

Van Fleet guided Florida to its biggest victory at the time, a stunning 16–6 win over Alabama in 1923, and had his team within a foot of the goal line at the end of the game in a 7–7 tie with Texas in Austin in 1924. Running back Bill Middlekauff was stopped just short as time expired.

Once Van Fleet's Army ROTC obligation was finished at UF, he left for duty in the Panama Canal Zone but used his military leave to coach the team in 1924. He died September 23, 1992, at the age of 100 and is buried at Arlington National Cemetery.

The Big One

It was a cold and wet day on November 29, 1923, when the Florida football team showed up in Birmingham, Alabama, for what was sure to be a beating. The Alabama Crimson Tide, coached by Wallace Wade, had already clinched the Southern Conference championship.

But Florida stopped Alabama five times inside the UF 10-yard line, and the underdogs won 16–6. Edgar Jones scored all of Florida's points—a field goal and touchdown runs of 12 and 20 yards.

Coach James Van Fleet employed two strategies in the hard-fought game. The leggings of his starters were soaked with rain and mud, so he had his starting players switch leggings with the backups at the half. And he kept an extra blocker in the game to help Ark Newton get off his punts.

"We Are the Boys"

One of the first songs the Florida band had to learn when it was formed was a number written by Bob Swanson and John Icenhour: "We Are the Boys." Today, it's a staple of Game Day, played between the third and fourth quarters.

One of the great traditions at Florida is the singing of a song that was written by one of the players on the team. There are several songs that are very similar to "We Are the Boys," including one written in Toledo, Ohio, by Joseph Murphy in 1906. But Bob Swanson, a tackle on the 1920 team, is given credit with penning the ditty in 1919 with the help of student and founder of the Original University Jazz Band, John Icenhour.

Swanson wrote the song for his barbershop group, The Prickly Heat Quartet. The song was first performed at a game in 1924, but it wasn't until the 1930s that fans began swaying back and forth to the tune.

Gator fans through the years have added their own touches (noted in parentheses at right), and the song has become a big part of Game Day in Gainesville.

We are the boys from old Florida
F-L-O-R-I-D-A
Where the girls are the fairest,
The boys are the squarest
Of any old state down our way (Hey!)
We are all strong for old Florida
Down where the old Gators play (Go Gators!)
In all kinds of weather
We'll all stick together
For F-L-O-R-I-D-A (Go Gators!)

Florida fans also have added a long lean during a drawn-out "to-geth-eeerrrr" as they sway with arms locked around shoulders in the stands.

Songs Galore

The names Thornton Whitney Allen and Milton Yeats may not be in the football record books, but they play a big part in every game at UF.

Yeats, who was a member of the University Quartet, wrote the school's alma mater in 1925. Allen is credited as the writer of the Florida fight song, which goes by two titles—"The Orange and Blue" and "On, Brave Old Florida"—that same year.

The alma mater is sung before games and then again after Gator wins, followed by the fight song. This was a tradition started by coach Urban Meyer in 2005. He takes the entire team to the Gator band and they sing along. Until Meyer's arrival, few people knew there were words to the fight song.

Coach in Waiting

When James Van Fleet left Florida to return to the military, he handpicked his successor in old friend and assistant coach H. L. "Tom" Sebring. Where Van Fleet believed in defense, Sebring liked to open things up offensively, and his teams showed it.

Sebring, a former Kansas State star, came to Florida to enter law school. He eventually graduated and went on to serve a distinguished career in that field. He served as a judge during the Nuremberg Trials, was a chief justice in the Florida Supreme Court, and eventually served as the dean of the Stetson Law School in Deland, Florida. Sebring also had a degree in architecture.

With the players left over from Van Fleet's recruiting, Sebring guided his first Gator team in 1925 to an 8–2 record, in part because he allowed All-Southern Conference quarterback Edgar Jones to call his own plays.

Jones responded with what was a school-record 108 points, as Florida won eight games for the first time ever.

The only losses were to Georgia Tech in Atlanta and Alabama in Montgomery. But with many of the Van Fleet stars graduated, the Gators went 2–6–2 during the 1926 season, losing five straight games at one point.

Sebring got it turned around the following year, but the 1927 season did include an embarrassing 12–0 loss to Davidson College in Gainesville on October 1. The following week, his team would make history.

Behind "Goof" Bowyer's 44-yard touchdown run and two scores by Clyde Crabtree, Florida won at Auburn for the first time ever on October 8 by a score of 33–6. The Gators also got revenge for a pair of lopsided losses to Alabama under Sebring by winning 13–6 in Montgomery.

Sebring left to pursue his law career after the 1927 season, yet the stage was set for one of the greatest Gator seasons ever the following year.

General James Van Fleet's successor, Tom Sebring, won 17 games in 3 years and left a rugged squad behind for the next coach, Charles Bachman.

H. L. "Tom" Sebring believed Florida had to crank up its offense and had the players to do it. UF went 7–3 in 1927, and the following year under Charles Bachman the Gators led the nation in scoring.

Van Sickel: UF's First Superstar

The new Gateway of Champions at Florida Field has granite blocks at the entrance, each one telling the story of a player who was named an All-American for the Gators. The first one—and there can only be one first—belongs to the late Dale Harris Van Sickel, who played end from 1927 to '29.

Dale Van Sickel was an end for both the offense and defense from 1927 to '29, and in 1928 he was named Florida's first All-American. Van Sickel was inducted into the College Football Hall of Fame in 1975.

Van Sickel played almost 60 minutes of every game during his career at Florida and played with a sense of abandonment. A ball thrown in the air belonged to him and only him. His sure hands and quick feet allowed him to become a crucial offensive weapon on some of the best Gator teams, including a 1928 team that led the nation in scoring.

Van Sickel was a star on both offense and defense, but it was his pass-catching ability that earned him the honor of All-American. Florida became more of a passing team during his career, in part because of Van Sickel's ability.

Van Sickel was inducted into the College Football Hall of Fame in 1975, and in his official Hall of Fame biography, UF coach Charles Bachman is quoted as saying Van Sickel was "the greatest all-around end I've ever seen."

Movie Time

After serving as a basketball and track coach following his football career at UF, Dale Van Sickel went to Hollywood to pursue a career in the movies. He began a long stint as a stunt man, playing in such television serials as *The Roy Rogers Show,* and went on to appear in movies such as *Duck Soup* and *Spartacus.*

His specialties were fight scenes and car stunts, and often studios would cast certain leading men because of their resemblance to Van Sickel. The All-American appeared in more than 200 movies and television shows, with his last appearance in the TV movie *Duel* in 1971.

Van Sickel was founder and first president of the Stuntmen's Association of Motion Pictures in 1961. He passed away in California in 1977.

Star Struck

Ark Newton, here carried off the field on the shoulders of Gator fans, was one of the best players to wear orange and blue during the 1920s. Newton was the captain of the 1924 team and deadly with his punting and dropkicks.

Although Florida football began in 1906, it was during the 1920s that the program began to produce players who would gain national notoriety. In addition to Dale Van Sickel, the school's first All-American, this decade gave rise to three of the greatest early Gators of all time: R. D. "Ark" Newton, Edgar Jones, and Clyde "Cannonball" Crabtree.

Newton, from Camden, Arkansas, showed up on campus to see if Florida was the right fit and was dragged to practice by another star of the era, 230-pound guard Carl "Tootie" Perry. When Newton boomed a punt over everyone's head, he was offered a scholarship. Captain of the 1924 team, he was a weapon as a punter in an era where field position was vital. He also drop-kicked field goals and was a threat to score from anywhere on the field.

Jones, who succeeded Newton as captain in 1925, was an All-Southern selection at quarterback and scored a school record 108 points as a senior. In 1923 he scored all 16 points in a win over Alabama. He threw for Florida's only score in 1924 in a tie at Texas. He returned to the school in 1930 to serve as athletic director.

Crabtree, a member of Florida's "Phantom Four" backfield in 1928, could pass with either hand and kick with either foot. In a win over Auburn in 1927, he ran for two touchdowns and had a pair of punts over 50 yards, one with each foot. Crabtree, a 5'8" quarterback, allowed Florida to roll the play in either direction because of his ambidexterity.

One of the top Gators during the 1920s was a 5' 10", 230-pound guard named Carl Perry who went by the nickname "Tootie." Perry played every minute of every game, and his specialty was blocking punts.

Coach Charley

Charles Bachman, here instructing Gators Jimmy Steele and Hal Betten, turned Florida into an offensive dynamo during his first three seasons at UF. He won 16 of his first 19 games as the Gators' head coach.

Royce Good-bread (left) and Carl Brumbaugh (center) helped form Florida's "Phantom Four" backfield that worked behind an outstanding line, which included Tom "Bull" Fuller (right) in 1928.

Charles Bachman was a football man. He played at the University of Notre Dame under the legendary Knute Rockne from 1914 to 1916 and coached at both Northwestern and Kansas State, where he spent eight years before being lured to Florida. While at Kansas State he developed improved padding for the players' uniforms and was a big believer in off-season workouts to get, and keep, his team in shape.

The University of Florida was attractive to Bachman, in part because the humid climate of Florida would be better for his wife's asthma. Bachman was hired to be the Gators' coach after Tom Sebring resigned following the 1927 football season. He inherited plenty of solid talent from Sebring—players such as Clyde Crabtree, Wilbur James, Red Bethea, and Dale Van Sickel, to name a few—and forged one of the greatest seasons in Florida football's history his first year as coach, when the 1928 team went 8–1. Bachman was a big believer in offensive football, and he was the first Florida coach to ever beat Georgia, winning 26–6 in Savannah on November 10, 1928.

Bachman finished with a record of 22–6–1 in his first three seasons at Florida, but he then struggled in his final two when the last of the talent left behind by coach Sebring had graduated. The Gators won only five games in 1931 and '32, which included a close game against Auburn (13–12) on October 24, 1931. When Bachman's five-year contract with the university was up, he bolted for Michigan State.

One Point Away

The great 1928 team included such stars as Royce Goodbread, shown here making a toss during practice at the beach.

lorida has won three national championships to date and has had plenty of great teams in its amazing history. But the football team that should be in all conversations about "the greatest ever" should be the one from 1928, Charles Bachman's first season as head coach.

That team steamrolled opponents behind the "Phantom Four" backfield of Clyde "Cannonball" Crabtree, Royce Goodbread, Carl Brumbaugh, and Rainey Cawthon. The Florida Gators led the nation that year in scoring and outscored their opponents 336–44.

Brumbaugh, the quarterback of the 1928 team, even made the popular newspaper feature *Ripley's Believe It Or Not* by scoring three touchdowns in two minutes during a 27–0 win over Auburn on October 13. Brumbaugh ran 19 yards for a touchdown, scored on a 30-yard run after an Auburn player fumbled, and ran an interception back 36 yards in a scoring avalanche. He also kicked the extra point after his final touchdown of the game.

FLORIDA 1928 NATIONAL HIGH SCORING CHAMPIONS 336-44

The Gators beat Georgia for the first time during the 1928 season, scoring in every quarter in front of a crowd of more than 15,000 in Savannah. Among the other wins for this outstanding team were a 73–0 smashing of Mercer in Gainesville for Florida's homecoming game, a 71–6 trampling of Sewanee in Jacksonville, and a 60–6 victory over Washington and Lee University, also in Jacksonville.

But the too-good-to-be-true season ended on a down note when the Gators lost at Tennessee 13–12 on December 8 after missing both extra points. Coach Bachman had used his best Knute Rockne impression, waving a telegram in front of the team before the game and saying the Rose Bowl was considering inviting Florida to the big game if the Gators won. He later admitted he knew Georgia Tech already had the bid.

During the Tennessee game, a wet field slowed down the usually speedy Gator backs. Whether the Volunteers wet the field before the game or it simply froze over and then thawed into a mushy mess is still up for speculation to this day.

The 1928 Florida team led the nation in scoring with 336 points and came 1 point away from an undefeated season. The Gators' lone loss came in the last game of the season at Tennessee 13–12, when UF missed both extra points on a muddy field.

New Digs

When John J. Tigert, a former head coach at Kentucky and a Rhodes scholar, became the president of the University of Florida in 1928, nobody could have anticipated the impact he would have on the football program.

He was instrumental in forming the Southeastern Conference and began the practice of offering athletic scholarships to cover tuition, board, and books. But his biggest contribution was the building of a stadium that years later would be known simply as "The Swamp."

And it was a swamp. Tigert picked a site on campus that was a waterlogged depression in the ground and hired UF architecture dean Rudolph Weaver to design the stadium. Tigert was convinced that Florida would never get anywhere in football without its own stadium, but the trick was to put the money together without using state funds. The state of Florida was reeling financially from the Great

UF president John J. Tigert, watching a Gator game here with other dignitaries in 1928, was one of the most influential people in Gator football history. He was instrumental in getting a stadium built and starting the Southeastern Conference.

Depression on top of a 1928 hurricane that had destroyed much of the state's sugar industry.

But Tigert was undaunted. He pulled together ten friends and raised the $118,000 needed for the project. Ground was broken on April 16, 1930, and 32 rows of seating were built on the north, east, and west sides despite drainage issues that turned the ground into mud during digging. There was no track put around the field to allow fans to be closer to the action.

The 21,769-seat stadium was ready for play on November 8, 1930, and Alabama's national championship team christened it with a 20–0 victory over the Gators. Today, anyone entering the stadium at ground level is standing on row 32.

Tigert Hall, which is the main administrative building on the Florida campus, is named for the man who had an incredible influence on both the university and the Gator Nation.

Today it is known as "The Swamp," but when construction started in April 1930 on Florida's new football stadium, it truly was a swamp. Workers had to keep draining water from the depression where the field was built to allow construction to continue.

Game Day Comes Together

As Florida football continued to grow, cheerleaders became a part of the Game Day experience. Fans could buy programs to follow along with the cheers yelled by these six male cheerleaders. New stadium, band, cheerleaders… this was major college football.

As Florida's football program started to become a national power during the 1920s, fan support grew enormously. The hundreds of fans who used to perch on the hoods of their cars to watch the Gators play at Fleming Field turned into thousands sitting in temporary bleachers and eventually filling the new stadium starting in 1930. The Florida Land Boom meant a huge influx of new residents for the Sunshine State and, therefore, new fans.

It wasn't unusual for fans to walk with the team to the downtown train station to cheer them on to a road trip or fill University Avenue after a big road victory. This era was also the beginning of homecoming games. They started as something called "Dad's Day" and morphed into the first homecoming game played against Drake on November 27, 1924. By then, Florida had enough alumni to entice back to Gainesville to celebrate not only the current Gators but also their years at the fledgling university.

As the school grew from two buildings to six, the student population grew as well, and by the time the Gators started playing in their new stadium, the crowd was serenaded by a 70-piece marching band.

"THEY ARE OFF." 12/6/28.

Sweater-clad male cheerleaders also had become a part of Game Day in Gainesville, leading the crowds in orchestrated yells to give the team some life. Fans could pay 25 cents for a program that contained the different cheers to use during the games.

It had even become fashionable for politicians to be seen at the games, so the Florida governor and state senators began to show up from Tallahassee to see the Gators play. Those who were not able to attend had another way to follow the team at selected games: Beginning with the Auburn game on October 13, 1928, games were broadcast on the radio.

As Florida's undefeated football team makes its way to the train station, students flood University Avenue to send the team on its way. Two days later in Knoxville, Tennessee, Florida would suffer its only loss of the season.

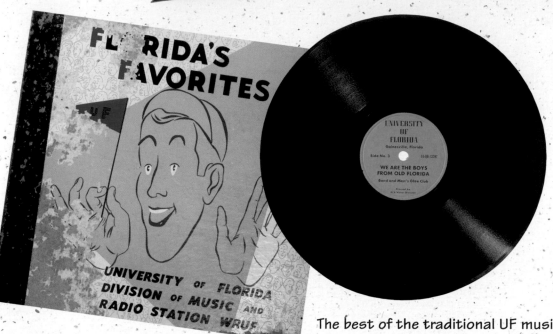

ALUMNUS, October, 1931

"Fighting Gators" of '31

PROBABLY never before in history has there been such universal interest on the part of the people of Florida in our football here at the University. Sam Butz, the genial sports editor of the Jacksonville *Times-Union* told me early in September that in spite of the fact that our prospects for a winning team were not bright, yet the people of Florida were reconciled to conditions as they are and were showing more interest than ever. What our friends wanted to know most was, who would be the likely candidates for the team and what could they do.

I believe the interest in Florida football has gradually been increasing with the years, and will continue to increase as the people more and more become better acquainted with the accomplishments of the University. Academically and athletically our school is becoming better known and with it has developed a pride of ownership that augurs well for the future growth of the university.

When I arrived on the campus in the Fall of 1928 I immediately announced that it was my intention to do my utmost to give Florida the best football teams possible and to schedule games with the best teams that could be obtained so that the people of Florida could see in their own state representative teams from all sections of the country. Generally speaking, I believe both of these objectives have been attained. Our teams of 1928-29-30 have made outstanding records and have brought national prominence to our school. Our schedules have become increasingly difficult each year as such schools as Ga. Tech, Alabama, North Carolina, Oregon, Chicago, Syracuse, Harvard and the University of California at Los Angeles were added.

Last Saturday after the North Carolina game I met Frank Simmons of Syracuse who was here to scout Florida. He told me that the spirit of our team and our student body was an inspiration to him, and that the phrase "Fighting Gators" was a name we richly deserved.

As everyone who has followed the Gators in recent years will recall, the team of 1930 was made up for the most part of seniors backed up by inadequate reserves. We had one fine team, but when it became necessary to substitute, except in one or two positions, our team strength was greatly weakened. The Tennessee game last year saw the curtain drop on such outstanding players as Capt. "Red" Bethea, Jimmy Steele, Ed Sauls,

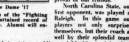

CHARLIE BACHMAN, Notre Dame '17

In his fourth year as head coach of the "Fighting Gators". Over past three seasons attained record of 22 victories; six defeats and one tie. Alumni will enjoy this article by Coach Bachman.

"Muddy" Waters, Ben Clemons, Frank Clark and Wilbur James. Following the winter semester examinations Carlos Proctor dropped out of school and late in the spring Florida football stock took another nose dive when it became known that Luke Dorsett, alternate captain and quarterback, would not return for the 1931 season.

To start the current season we had only three regulars of the year before. Added to this number were a small group of reserves, including some of the members of the "Omelet" Squad, and a rather large number of players from the freshman squad. From the opening day of practice it was obvious that while we would not have an outstanding team this year from the point of view of victories, we at least would have a rather large group of players who were eager to learn, were willing to make the sacrifice necessary to develop team play and team spirit, and above all they were mentally alert and the type who could be depended upon to obey the letter and the spirit of the training rules. It is already over a month and a half since fall training started and two games have already been played and the fine spirit which was so encouraging from the start has continued. Although we probably will not win very many games against our more experienced opponents, I feel that our team will give the best they have and that their efforts will meet with the approval of our friends.

North Carolina State, our first opponent, was played at Raleigh. In this game our players not only surprised themselves, but their coach as well by their splendid team work, their vicious tackling and blocking and by their mental alertness which turned scoring opportunities into touchdowns.

The second game on our schedule was played on Florida Field against the Tarheels of North Carolina. History now records this game as a 0 to 0 tie game which was one of those heartbreaking exhibitions in which the ticking of the watch became the most important part of the game as in the closing minutes of the game North Carolina for the third time during the game had the ball inches away from our goal line. While the offense failed to click in the North Carolina game, the defense was all that was desired. Offensive play requires experienced players, natural ability, perfect timing and execution, and mental poise, most of which comes from experience. Defense on the

(Turn to page 22)

9

The best of the traditional UF music included "We Are The Boys," "Dixie Medley," and "Orange and Blue," which can all be found on this vintage album, *Florida's Favorites.*

The stadium where Florida plays football has been around since 1930, but the place wasn't called "The Swamp" until the 1992 season when Coach Steve Spurrier came up with the name.

Charles Bachman played for Knute Rockne at Notre Dame and coached at Northwestern and Kansas State before he was lured to Florida in 1928. Bachman coached the Gators for five seasons and produced some of the school's finest early teams.

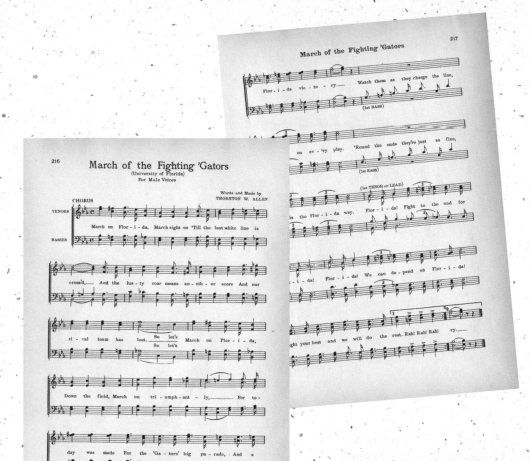

As Florida football began to grow, so did the crowds. By the mid-1920s, the university had enough alumni to have a homecoming game, and the first one was against Drake on November 27, 1924. Florida sent the alumni home happy with a 10–0 win.

Some of the songs of the era would not be considered politically correct today. But there was no shortage of tunes for Florida alumni at sing-a-longs, including this ditty by Thornton Allen.

This postcard provides a nice view of the newly erected Florida Field in 1930, surrounded by the university's lush land and campus buildings.

THE SLIDE BACK

1933–1949

While Florida football had risen to national prominence in the 1920s, it was about to fall on hard times. Pay was cut for coaches and athletic administrators, and northern schools began to raid the state for speedy backs. From 1933 through '49, the Gators managed only three winning seasons. These were tough times.

There have been many incarnations of the Gator mascot, but long before Albert was introduced, students put together this rough version of an alligator made from wood and powered by legs—human legs, that is.

After having so much success early in his career, Charles Bachman's last two teams struggled, winning only five games. The highlight of those two seasons was a 12–2 win over UCLA in Gainesville.

Birth of a League

The SEC has shown incredible growth since its inception and has turned the SEC Championship Game into the model for all other conferences to follow. Florida won this one over Alabama in 2008 at the Georgia Dome.

Sometimes, too much of a good thing can be bad. And that's how one of the most powerful conferences in college sports was formed.

The Southeastern Conference (SEC) can trace its roots back to 1894 and the formation of the Southern Intercollegiate Athletic Association (SIAA)—the first collegiate athletic conference formed in the United States. Florida was a member of the SIAA when it started playing football. That conference started with seven teams and grew to 30 by 1920.

At a meeting in Gainesville on December 12, 1920, the Southern Conference came about when 14 schools, including Florida, split from the SIAA. By 1932, the conference had 23 members, including many of the schools that now are in the Atlantic Coast Conference, and had become too big to have competitive balance.

At the Southern Conference's annual meeting in Knoxville, Tennessee, on December 12 and 13, 1932, the SEC was born. Florida president John J. Tigert was at the forefront of the movement to pare down the Southern Conference into a more manageable 13 teams. Tigert, whose influence on the Florida football program was so powerful that he was named one of the ten most influential people in the program's history by *The Gainesville Sun* in 2007,

was named chairman of the Committee of Presidents. This group came up with the more compact conference idea. Tigert was asked to be the SEC's first president but declined because of financial problems that needed his attention at the University of Florida.

The decision was made to limit the Southeastern Conference to schools that were south and west of the Appalachian Mountains. The new conference would make travel easier and less expensive. Florida's first SEC game was played on October 7, 1933, when the Gators beat Sewanee 31–0 in Jacksonville. Florida finished with a 2–3 record in its first year in the conference.

UF president John J. Tigert (center) was one of the key figures in forming the Southeastern Conference. He was chairman of the Committee of Presidents that came up with the new 13-team league in 1932.

The Original 13

University of Alabama Crimson Tide (Tuscaloosa, AL)

Auburn University Tigers (Auburn, AL)

University of Florida Gators (Gainesville, FL)

University of Georgia Bulldogs (Athens, GA)

Georgia Tech Yellow Jackets (Atlanta, GA)

University of Kentucky Wildcats (Lexington, KY)

Louisiana State University Tigers (Baton Rouge, LA)

University of Mississippi Rebels (Oxford, MS)

Mississippi State University Bulldogs (Starkville, MS)

Sewanee Tigers (Sewanee, TN)

University of Tennessee Volunteers (Knoxville, TN)

Tulane University Green Wave (New Orleans, LA)

Vanderbilt University Commodores (Nashville, TN)

Over the years, the SEC has undergone several changes and now sports 12 schools, 10 of which are charter members. Sewanee in Tennessee withdrew in 1940 after having never won an SEC game. Georgia Tech pulled out in 1964, followed by Tulane in 1966.

In 1992, the conference expanded to 12 teams with the additions of South Carolina and Arkansas. The addition of these teams was the brainchild of then-SEC commissioner Roy Kramer, who wanted to allow the conference to play a championship game and reap the rewards of the extra revenue. The NCAA had passed a rule that a conference with 12 teams could have a championship game.

The SEC did not have a commissioner until 1940, when the office was created and Martin S. Conner took the job. N. W. Dougherty was acting commissioner in 1946 and was followed by Bernie Moore, Tonto Coleman, Dr. Boyd McWhorter, Dr. Harvey Schiller, Roy Kramer, and current SEC commissioner Mike Slive.

From its humble beginnings, the conference has grown into a giant, filling its stadiums with enormous crowds each year. The league has led college football in percentage of attendance every year since the statistic started being kept in 1983.

"The World's Largest Outdoor Cocktail Party"

Florida and Georgia began playing on an intermittent basis in 1915 (although Georgia claims a victory in 1905 before UF officially started playing football), and the games were played in several cities—Athens, Georgia; Tampa, Florida; Savannah, Georgia; and even once in Gainesville. Three times it was played at the Gator Bowl in Jacksonville, which is now Jacksonville Municipal Stadium, prior to the two teams becoming charter members of the SEC.

But once the league was formed, the rivalry heated up. The two schools began making Florida–Georgia an annual affair in Jacksonville starting in 1933. The only two times the game was not played in Jacksonville were in 1994 and '95 when the Gator Bowl was being renovated to become the home of the new NFL team coming to town—the Jacksonville Jaguars. In those years the game was played first in Gainesville and then in Athens.

Each school receives half of the tickets, and until the stadium's renovation, fans of the two schools were seated in adjacent sections at each side of the 50-yard line and behind both goalposts. After the renovation, fans were divided in the end zones, cutting down the chances for confrontation.

The game began to be known as "The World's Largest Outdoor Cocktail Party" when sports columnist Bill Kastelz coined the name in the 1950s after observing all of the tailgate parties on his way to the press box.

The game is so big that it even has its own hall of fame. In 1996, the Jacksonville Sports Organizing Committee came up with the idea and inducted its first class—Kerwin Bell, Ray Graves, Shane Matthews, and Lee McGriff from Florida and Vince Dooley, Rodney Hampton, Buck Belue, and Frankie Sinkwich from Georgia.

Georgia dominated the first several games, winning seven in a row from 1941 to 1948. But its history has included a series of streaks. Florida won four in a row from

Steve Spurrier's senior season was marred by a devastating loss to Georgia in 1966, but he would get his revenge as the Florida head coach 30 years later, beating the Bulldogs 11 of 12 times.

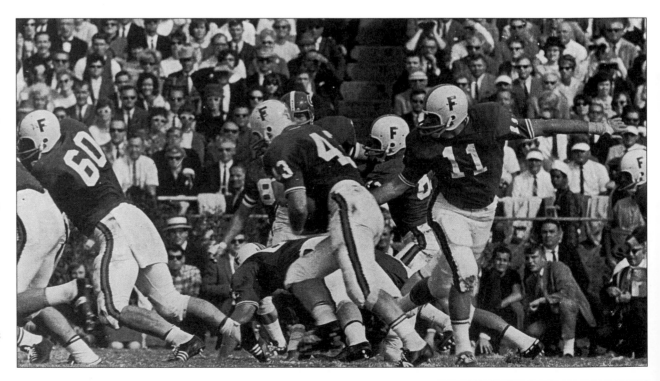

Florida and Georgia already had a heated rivalry before the game was moved to Jacksonville in 1933 and eventually became "The World's Largest Outdoor Cocktail Party." The game even has its own hall of fame.

went for it on fourth-and-one from his own 29. Headlines around the state the next day read, "Fourth and Dumb."

The 1980s belonged to the Bulldogs, who beat UF the first time Florida was No. 1 in the nation in 1985. The 1980 game is the most famous in the series' history because of Belue's 93-yard touchdown pass to Lindsay Scott with 1:13 to play, breaking the hearts of Gators everywhere. Spurrier arrived as coach in 1990, and everything changed. His Gators would win 11 of 12 games, including the one game that was played in Athens, a 52–17 embarrassment for Georgia.

Ron Zook, Spurrier's successor, continued the winning ways of the Gators with victories in his first two Florida–Georgia games, losing his last one the week he was fired. Urban Meyer won his first two against the Bulldogs but lost in 2007 in a controversial game that saw Georgia's players rush the field after the Bulldogs' first score. The Gators responded in 2008 with a 49–10 rout and a celebration of their own, as Meyer called two timeouts in the final minute of play, allowing fans and players extra time to take in the sweet victory.

The rivals have each had exciting wins in the series, but the 2007 game was especially memorable. The Bulldogs rushed the field after their first touchdown, and UF lost 14–7.

1955 to 1958 and another four straight from 1960 to '63 under Graves. But Graves also suffered two of the most infamous losses during that decade. In 1966, the unbeaten Gators came in with the eventual Heisman Trophy winner, Steve Spurrier, and were hammered 27–10. And in 1968, when Graves switched his offensive and defensive coordinator to give the team some spark, Georgia responded with a 51–0 win.

Back-to-back games in the 1970s came down to two-point conversions. In 1974, Florida's Don Gaffney hit tight end Hank Foldberg for the game-winner but failed to complete the two-point try the following year in a 17–16 loss. In 1976, Georgia rallied from a 27–13 half-time deficit in part because Florida coach Doug Dickey

Dutch Treat

When Charles Bachman left Florida following the 1932 season, it was the beginning of difficult times at Florida. Because of the struggling economy, school president John J. Tigert had to cut the salaries of his athletic staff. That included the head football coach.

When he left, Bachman was making $7,500 a year. He recommended assistant D. K. "Dutch" Stanley, a 26-year-old former Florida end. Stanley was paid only $3,600 a year, which forced the Florida football coach to take a second job laying bricks for the Works Progress Administration to make ends meet.

Stanley's first team got off to a good start, with three wins and a tie against NC State in Raleigh. Three tough losses to Tennessee, Georgia, and Georgia Tech followed before Florida closed with wins over Auburn at the homecoming game and Maryland in Tampa.

Stanley's second season saw Florida go 6–3–1 and pull two big upsets. On November 17, 1934, the Gators went to Montgomery, Alabama, and knocked off Auburn 14–7.

A week later for homecoming, Florida beat Georgia Tech 13–12, coming back from a 12–0 halftime deficit thanks in part to a blocked punt by Alton Brown.

The next season would be Stanley's last. The Gators beat Stetson and Sewanee but lost five in a row in between. This time, Auburn and Georgia Tech would not be upset, instead winning by a combined score of 66–12. Before his last game against South Carolina in Tampa on December 7, 1935, Stanley read a story to the team from the *Tampa Tribune* that said he would be out as coach. The Gators rallied around their coach to win 22–0.

Stanley returned to the school in 1946 to become the head of the department of physical education.

Florida opened its 1935 season with a 34–0 win over Stetson in Gainesville on September 28. Here, Hub McAnly fights for yardage against the Stetson defense.

D. K. "Dutch" Stanley (center) seemed to have things headed in the right direction with a 6–3–1 season in 1934. But the following season would be his last after a 3–7 mark that included five straight losses.

Cody Couldn't Cut It

The Josh Cody era was not a high point in Florida football. The games were dull with almost no offense, and an FBI investigation didn't help. Cody (right) lasted only four seasons, losing 24 games.

When Florida athletic director and former Gator quarterback Edgar Jones went looking for a new football coach following the 1935 season, he went to the Vanderbilt staff and tabbed Josh Cody, an assistant for the Commodores. Cody had a defense-first philosophy, and it showed over the next four seasons.

The trouble was the offense.

In his final season as Florida's coach in 1939, the Gators averaged seven points a game while allowing six points. The result was a mundane 5–5–1 record. Florida shut out five opponents that season, but the Gators were shut out three times and scored only a safety in a 6–2 loss to Georgia.

And that was the best year of the Cody era.

His first season saw Florida go 4–6; his second 4–7. There was some talent on the Florida campus, with players such as Walter Mayberry, Fergie Ferguson, and punter Bud Walton, who punted 23 times in a 0–0 tie with Georgia Tech in Atlanta in 1938. There just wasn't enough.

Cody also had to deal with a scandal involving some of his players who worked for the Works Progress Administration when the FBI investigated whether they were paid for work they did not do. No charges were filed, but the black mark on the program cost Cody the support of some of the university's biggest boosters. After compiling a four-year record of 17–24–2, Cody was not asked to return as Florida's coach.

One Big Win

While Josh Cody did not find much success as a Florida coach, he did have one spectacular highlight. On October 12, 1939, the Gators traveled to Boston to face Boston College at Fenway Park. BC coach Frank Leahy, who would go 19–1 in his two seasons at the school before moving on to Notre Dame, was so confident that he sat his first-team backfield at the start of the game.

Florida scored first on a 25-yard pass from Bud Walton to Leo Cahill in the first quarter. Leahy put his starters in the game, but the Florida defense, led by Fergie Ferguson, held onto the 7–0 lead for the rest of the afternoon. A four-touchdown underdog, the Gators stopped BC eight times deep in Florida territory.

Florida's defense was the story when the Gators traveled to Boston and handed Boston College its only loss of the year, 7–0. BC was able to move the ball against Florida but failed to score.

Call Him Fergie

Fergie Ferguson was as fine an athlete as Florida has ever seen, an All-America football player who was also a javelin and boxing champion. Ferguson held Florida's receiving records until the 1960s.

Florida was struggling to win games on the football field as the decade turned to the 1940s, but there was one player who was worth the price of admission. His name was Forrest K. "Fergie" Ferguson, a magnificent athlete from Stuart, Florida, who could do just about everything. That included throwing the javelin (national Amateur Athletic Union champion) and boxing (undefeated state champion).

But it was on the football field that Ferguson made a name for himself. He was good enough to be named Florida's second first-team All-American after he finished the 1941 season with five touchdown receptions.

Ferguson, who combined excellent speed with a powerful upper body, almost always played 60 minutes of every game and started every game he played in from 1939 to '41. In 1941, he caught 26 passes, the third-highest total in the nation that year. On defense, his specialty was tackling backs for losses. He caught both touchdown passes, one a 74-yarder, in a 14–0 win at Miami on November 15, 1941, and tackled Hurricanes for losses adding up to 67 yards. He also had an interception in the game.

Ferguson, who finished his career with 43 catches for 668 yards, also played for the Gator baseball team in his senior season. His receiving records stood at UF until the 1960s, when passing became a bigger part of college football.

Legacy of Bravery

When Fergie Ferguson left Florida, he immediately entered military service and fought in World War II as a second lieutenant. After the D-Day landing at Normandy in 1944, he was awarded the Distinguished Service Cross, the second-highest medal awarded for bravery under fire. But he was wounded during the landing and eventually died of those wounds ten years later.

In 1954, Florida began giving out the Fergie Ferguson Award to the senior player who displays outstanding leadership, character, and courage. Fullback Malcolm Hammock was the first winner, and it has since been presented to such Gator greats as Steve Spurrier, Jack Youngblood, Wes Chandler, and Kerwin Bell.

Among the Florida players who have received the Fergie Ferguson Award is Jack Youngblood, a member of the NFL Hall of Fame and the Gator Ring of Honor.

The Lieb Years

Florida went all the way to the West Coast to find its next coach after Josh Cody was let go after the 1939 season, tabbing Loyola Marymount head coach Thomas J. Lieb. A former Notre Dame tackle, Lieb would last through the 1945 season, producing only one winning record.

His first team was his best, going 5–5 and beating Georgia and Georgia Tech for the first time in the same season. The 18–13 win over Georgia on November 9, 1940, was sparked by a blocked punt by Fergie Ferguson that was returned for a score by end John Piombo. Piombo struck again two weeks later in Atlanta by returning an interception 71 yards for a touchdown in a 16–7 win over Tech.

But by 1941, many of Florida's players were leaving to fight in World War II. The 1941 team went 4–6 but did manage to stun unbeaten Miami 14–0 in front of a state-record crowd of 31,731 at the Orange Bowl.

Thomas J. Lieb (left) came to Florida from Loyola Marymount, and he paid early dividends. The Gators beat Georgia and Georgia Tech in 1940, the first time UF had beaten both schools in the same year.

The following year Lieb put his name in the record books. Unfortunately, it was for the wrong reason.

The Gators had lost three straight when they traveled to Jacksonville for the annual battle with Georgia. The Bulldogs were led by Heisman winner Frankie Sinkwich and All-America end George Poschner. When the November 7, 1942, game was over, Florida had been handed the worst loss in the school's history. Sinkwich accounted for four touchdowns rushing and passing despite playing sparingly in the 75–0 win for the Bulldogs.

There was no team in 1943 because of the war, and Lieb would eke out his only winning record the following year at 4–3. In 1945, the Gators went 4–5–1, but three of the wins were over Camp Blanding, Southwestern Louisiana, and Presbyterian College. Lieb's last game would be a 12–0 loss to the United States Amphibs.

Players on the Florida football team, here seated in the dugout at Florida Field, had some highlights during the years of Thomas Lieb, but there was also the worst loss in school history: 75–0 against Georgia.

Standouts of the Era

Not everybody gets a song written about them, but Florida halfback Charlie Hunsinger, who starred from 1946 through '49, can say he did.

Birmingham News sports editor Zipp Newman thought so highly of Hunsinger he penned "The Hunsinger Song," which included the lyrics, "Hunsinger's a humdinger not ever will he linger in ramming a ball thru the enemy's wall."

Hunsinger was an All-SEC player as a junior and senior and scored twice as Florida ended Georgia's seven-game winning streak in 1949. In a 1949 game against Furman University, he ran for 199 yards, which is still one of the top 10 performances in Gator history.

Another of the era's stars was Walter "Tiger" Mayberry, a tailback and defensive back from Daytona Beach, Florida, who in 1937 was the state's first All-SEC player. Mayberry became a Marine fighter pilot and was downed in the Pacific Theater in 1943. He was captured and died in a Japanese prison camp.

Tommy Harrison put up the kind of numbers a back would be proud of today. He passed for 1,170 yards and ran for 963 during his career from 1939 through '41. Bobby Forbes was named to All-SEC teams twice—as a freshman in 1944 to the third team

Florida had yet to have a first-team member of the All-SEC team before Walter Mayberry came to school. Nicknamed "Tiger," Mayberry was a tailback and defensive back.

Sportswriter Zipp Newman penned the words that immortalized Florida halfback Chuck Hunsinger. Hunsinger scored 12 touchdowns in 1939 and rushed for 774 yards.

and as a senior in 1947 to the second team—and has two of the longest runs in Gator history. His 80-yarder against Auburn in 1947 wasn't enough to prevent a 20–14 loss, but his 70-yard scamper on a trap play against 18th-ranked NC State that same year was the only Gator score in a 7–6 victory.

Jimmy Kynes, who would have two sons later play for Florida, was the last player to play 60 minutes in a game. He did it several times in 1949 when he became Florida's first All-SEC lineman.

The Golden Era that Wasn't

Raymond "Bear" Wolf was not the first choice to succeed Thomas Lieb following the 1945 season. Former coach Dutch Stanley, who had returned from Duke to be the dean of the College of Physical Education, first went after Oklahoma State coach Jim Lookabaugh, then Rice coach Jess Neely. Both turned him down.

Wolf had been the coach at North Carolina, where he was 38–17–3. The former baseball player, who had one major league at-bat with Cincinnati, needed a job after serving in the Navy and so he applied. Stanley chose Wolf, and the so-called "Golden Era" was about to begin for Florida football.

In his first season, the 1946 Gators went 0–9. Some were close (13–7 to Ole Miss in Jacksonville in the opener); some were not (47–12 to Auburn to close the season on

November 30). The Gators were outscored 264–104 in the nine games. One of the best players on the team—center/linebacker Jimmy Kynes—would later sarcastically refer to the Wolf years as the "Golden Era," and the team would get together annually to reminisce.

The streak didn't end with the finish of the 1946 season. Florida lost the first three games of 1947 and headed to Raleigh, North Carolina, to face 18th-ranked North Carolina State. On a trap play early in the game, the Wolfpack defense keyed on Charlie Hunsinger, and the ball went to Bobby Forbes, who ran 70 yards for the score. The Gator defense made it hold up, surviving a missed field goal at the end of the game to win 7–6. The streak was over.

That team finished 4–5–1, while the 1948 team was a respectable 5–5 with wins over Auburn and Miami. But after another 4–5–1 season that included four straight losses, Wolf was let go with a 13–24–2 mark.

Was it the "Golden Era" or "Golden Error"? Raymond "Bear" Wolf's Florida teams lost every game in 1946 and the first three the following year, but the players of that period still get together to swap stories.

Practice didn't make perfect for coach Wolf's teams, although his last two teams in 1948 and '49 won nine games combined, and his final team in '49 handled Georgia 28–7.

Still Building

Even with a team struggling on the field, Florida kept adding to Florida Field. Part of the renovation was adding to the west side of the stadium, now known as the alumni side, taking the capacity up to 40,116.

While Florida's football program struggled throughout the era that included coaches Josh Cody, Thomas Lieb, and Bear Wolf, interest in the Gators was still growing. In 1949, plans were drawn up to add more seats to the west side of the stadium. Those seats today are some of the most cherished by Gator boosters.

The renovation that included adding 11,200 seats to that side was finished in 1950, taking UF's stadium capacity up to 40,116. The extra revenue would help fund a program so cash-strapped that players wore the same equipment in games as they did in practice.

During this time Florida also played in front of its largest crowd to date when the Gators traveled to the Orange Bowl to face Miami in front of close to 57,000 fans on November 11, 1949. The annual game against Georgia in Jacksonville was growing as well. There was a crowd of 36,500 in the stands when Florida stunned Georgia 28–7 on November 5, 1949. The team carried Wolf off the field on their shoulders after the big win.

The football team had given the student body something to rally around even if it was treading water. Students came to Wolf's support with public rallies that helped him receive a one-year extension following the 1948 season.

When the Gators broke their 13-game losing streak at North Carolina State, students who had been listening to the game on WRUF radio poured onto University Avenue to celebrate. The era also marked the beginning of students decorating their sororities and fraternities the night before homecoming games, as well as the formation of the F Club, a group of alumni and fans who joined to support the team through thick and thin.

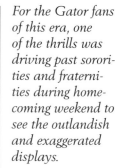

For the Gator fans of this era, one of the thrills was driving past sororities and fraternities during homecoming weekend to see the outlandish and exaggerated displays.

Stand Up and Holler

George Edmondson started the "Two Bits" cheer during a game against his alma mater, The Citadel. He did it for the last time in 2008 before a game against, of course, The Citadel.

Perhaps the best thing to come out of 1949 was the decision that Florida native George Edmondson made to attend a UF game against The Citadel, his alma mater. Edmondson was surprised to hear the Gators booed as they entered the field and chose to do something about it. He grabbed the friend who had come with him to the game and a few others in the stands and did the "Two Bits" cheer that was popular during the day.

It turned into a legend.

Soon known as "Mr. Two Bits," Edmondson would pop up at different places in the stands with his trademark orange sign and yellow shirt, whistle in mouth, and get the crowd going. For decades he ran around in the stadium leading the cheer. He started with a bugle but, according to Edmondson, "the bugle down through the years got a little cumbersome to carry around. So I started with the whistle."

Edmondson retired after the 1998 season and was presented with the game ball after the final home game by

Florida coach Steve Spurrier. He continued to make cameo appearances for big games, running out onto the field just before kickoff. Following Florida's final home game in 2008, ironically against The Citadel, he put down the whistle for good.

The Cheer

For George Edmondson, the evolution of the "Two Bits" cheer eventually would include a raised arm to start and then the throwing of arms as if signaling for a first down. In time, fans began to mimic him in the section where Edmondson was leading the yell.

Once he was established, Edmondson always wore the same outfit—a yellow shirt, an orange and blue tie, and light blue pants—to lead the cheer.

The old high school cheer is rarely used today except in Gainesville.

Two bits
Four bits
Six bits
A dollar
All for the Gators
Stand up and holler

For George Edmondson, it started out as a way to stop fans from booing the Gator players when they came onto the field. It turned him into a Gator icon, his "Two Bits" cheer becoming one of UF's most-loved traditions.

This postcard shows the Florida team preparing for its annual game against Georgia. The game has become a fixture in Jacksonville, where it is still played on an annual basis.

A cartoon in the *Orlando Morning Sentinel* in 1947 hit it right on the head: The legacy of John J. Tigert, who built the stadium and helped start the Southeastern Conference, would be difficult to live up to.

This playing card commemorates Fergie Ferguson, an incredible all-around athelete who played both ends of the field for Florida.

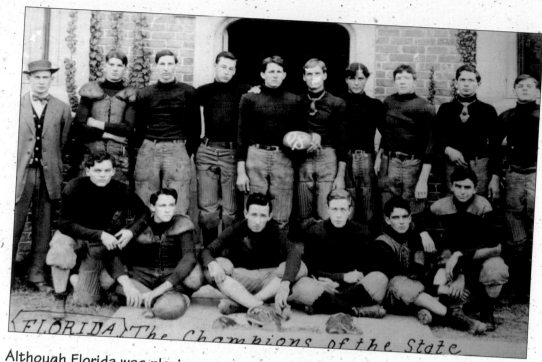

FLORIDA The Champions of the State

Although Florida was playing a national schedule, there was still room for games against in-state foes such as Miami and Tampa in the 1940s, as these state champions would attest.

It became a tradition for fans of the era to stick their ticket stubs in the band of their straw hats during the season as a show of loyalty to the program and the Gator Nation.

MARYLAND VS. FLORIDA

You can't tell the players without a program, and this one was for the 1935 homecoming game against Maryland on October 26. The Terrapins prevailed 20–6, the third of five straight losses for the Gators that season.

GETTING BETTER

1950–1969

After a dismal era of losing football teams, the next two decades would see Florida make a slow rise to national prominence. The Gators would play in their first bowl games, have their first Heisman Trophy winner, and become real contenders in the SEC. And they would do it with just two successful coaches instead of hiring a new coach every three or four years.

With Ray Graves coaching and a pair of quarterbacks slinging the ball, Florida became a consistent winner. Steve Spurrier (left) and Tommy Shannon were both effective and shared duties in 1964.

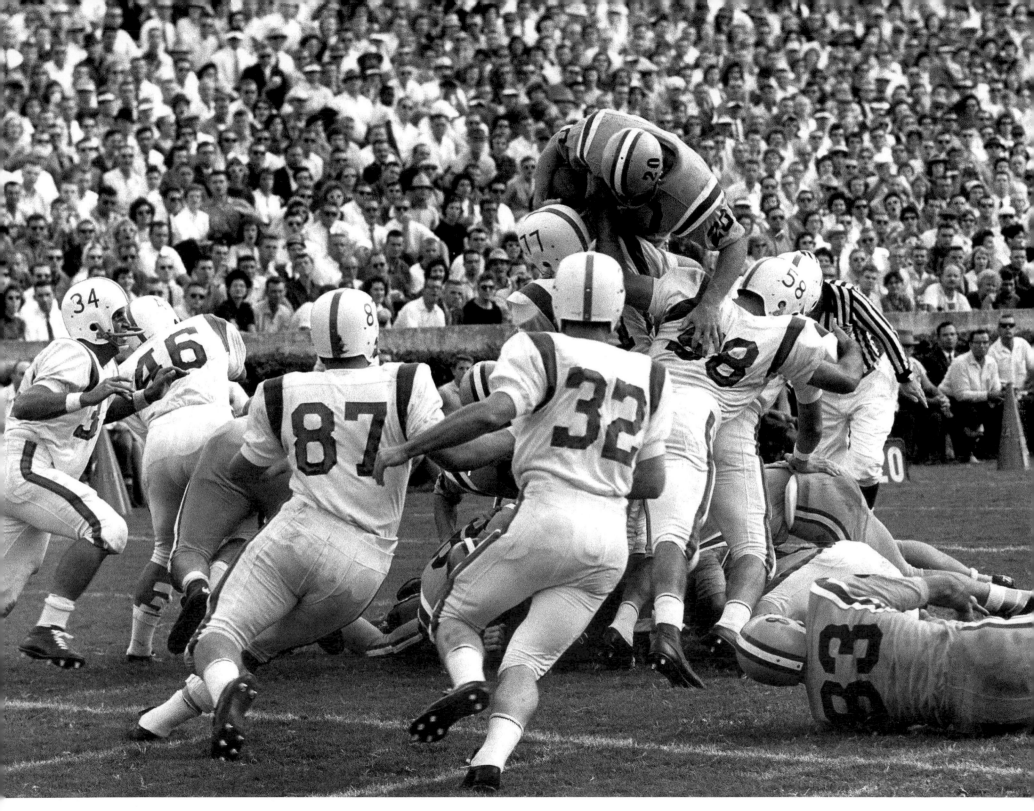

Florida defenders stop LSU's Heisman Trophy winner Billy Cannon (20) as he tries to go over the top in this 1959 homecoming game at Florida Field. Florida went 5–4–1 in Bob Woodruff's tenth and final season as head coach.

Big Bob

He was big.

He was burly.

At times, he was baffling.

He was Bob Woodruff, the 13th coach for the Florida football program.

When Red Sanders turned down Florida and stayed at UCLA, the school moved on to the former Tennessee lineman to change a program that had been mired in the mud of losing. And, boy, did he want change.

The meeting between Woodruff and the UF board lasted 12 hours before he was hired as coach and athletic director on January 6, 1950. Among the changes Woodruff wanted were to expand Florida's stadium, play all in-state games there, reorganize the Gator Boosters to allow the organization to raise more money, and create a department of intercollegiate athletics to be housed in the stadium.

"We had to have many things. . . . But, they agreed," Woodruff said. "They gave me just one order. They told me I had to beat Georgia." And he did—six out of ten times.

On the field, Woodruff made an immediate impact. On October 21, 1950, Florida went to Nashville and knocked off unbeaten

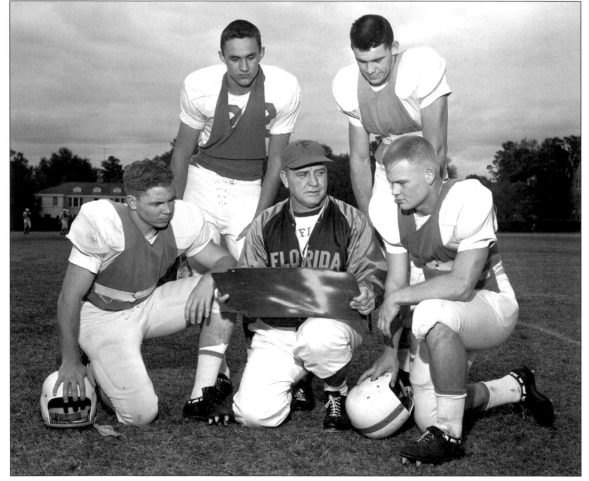

Bob Woodruff and his quarterbacks share a moment of strategy. Woodruff had only two losing teams in his ten seasons at UF, coached the Gators to their first bowl game, and started the series with Florida State.

Players and coaches watch the action during the 1958 Florida–Georgia game. Florida won 7–6 in Jacksonville. Bob Woodruff's orders when he took the UF coaching job included beating Georgia—and so he did . . . six times.

and 13th-ranked Vanderbilt 31–27. Loren Broadus was the hero of the game with 105 rushing yards, a touchdown catch, and two interceptions. With the win, Florida was ranked for the first time ever, coming in at No. 20 in the Associated Press poll.

The team, however, finished with four straight losses and a 5–5 record. Success, as Woodruff said when he took the job, would not come overnight.

That was shown again in 1951 when Florida went 5–5 for the second time in a row. But the finish was spectacular as the Gators beat Alabama in Tuscaloosa 30–21.

What followed was a season where Florida went to its first bowl game and finished the season 8–3. Woodruff, who was being paid $17,000 a year for the dual roles of coach and athletic director, seemed to have the Gators on the right track. Despite being a defense-minded coach, he opened up the offense at the suggestion of assistant Frank

Broyles, who would go on to be a successful head coach at Arkansas.

Florida players J. "Papa" Hall, Buford Long, Rick Casares, and Haywood Sullivan were making Florida football fun again. In 1950, Sullivan became the first sophomore in the SEC to throw for more than 1,000 yards, while the three halfbacks were adept at ripping off long runs at any moment.

Although Woodruff would hit a couple of potholes in his efforts to put Florida on the football map— 3–5–2 in 1953 and 4–6 in '55—his last four teams at UF went a combined 23–13–4. Most importantly, he had put the program on firm footing with upgraded facilities and financial security.

Woodruff also was the first coach to go against Florida State in 1958 and recorded some amazing wins during his ten seasons. The Gators always seemed to come up just a little short of winning an SEC championship and had many close-call losses during the decade.

Woodruff finished with a 5–4–1 record in 1959 and an overall mark that was 14 games over .500. He had improved the program, just not enough.

Another Yogi

Bob Woodruff often would have long periods of silence around his team. All-American Charlie LaPradd once said, "[They] would make you wonder if he was 30 minutes ahead of his listeners or 30 minutes behind."

But when he talked, well, Woodruff once described himself as "the oratorical equivalent to a blocked punt." His battle cry was "Oski Wow-Wow!" to be yelled by the team after a big play. Later in college football, "Oski" would become the signal to defenders that there had been an interception on the field.

Before Florida took the field against Tennessee in 1952, Woodruff told his Gators, "Boys, above all things, remember we're not beat yet." And before the Georgia game the year before, "Boys, remember the team that makes the fewest mistakes makes the fewest mistakes."

1951: A Special Season

Haywood Sullivan (left), with captain Angus Williams (center) and Kent Stevens, was the first sophomore in SEC history to pass for more than 1,000 yards. Sullivan left after the 1950 season to sign with the Boston Red Sox.

After Florida finished the 1951 season with a win over Alabama and the Gators were greeted by thousands of fans at the airport, there was talk about next year being special.

And it was. But not without a hitch.

Star quarterback Haywood Sullivan, who was an all-conference catcher on the baseball team, signed with the Boston Red Sox for a $75,000 bonus. Florida moved halfback Rick Casares to quarterback, but he felt uncomfortable at the position. A gut-wrenching 17–14 loss to Georgia Tech in the second game made the Florida coaches decide on a change. So the Gators turned to safety Doug Dickey, who in 1970 would become the head coach at UF, to be the new quarterback.

Despite the loss of Sullivan, Florida's offense thrived, with Casares, J. "Papa" Hall, and Buford Long providing

Going Bowling

Florida's first-ever sanctioned bowl game was played in a familiar place—Jacksonville's Gator Bowl, where the Gators had been playing Georgia every year since 1933. And Florida looked comfortable at the outset, jumping to a 14–0 lead over Tulsa.

UF got a break when Rick Casares missed an extra point and Tulsa was called offsides; Casares made the second try. He also scored on a two-yard run, and Fred Robinson hit J. "Papa" Hall on a 37-yard pass on fourth down for the other score.

Tulsa stormed back with a score in the third quarter and another in the fourth. But Tulsa kicker Tom Miner missed the second point after and also missed a late field goal, giving Florida the win in front of an estimated crowd of 28,000 on New Year's Day, 1953.

the firepower. Dickey rarely threw and instead tried to manage the game. The result was one of the best seasons in UF history up to that point. The Gators hammered Georgia 30–0, with Casares rushing for 108 yards and kicking a field goal.

Florida then received its first bowl bid with one game left in the season—a game they would go on to win, beating Kentucky, coached by Paul "Bear" Bryant, 27–0. The final record for the season was 8–3 after the 1953 Gator Bowl win over Tulsa.

Doug Dickey

He was raised in Gainesville and went to Florida to play quarterback. Doug Dickey excelled on the field and eventually came back to Florida as the head coach in 1970. Dickey is a member of the College Football Hall of Fame.

Scene of the Party

Female cheerleaders became the norm at Florida in the 1950s, adding to the enjoyment of a typical Game Day at Florida Field.

There's a theory that a lot of the people who attend college football games don't go for the football but for everything that surrounds it. That was certainly the case for some Gator fans during the 1950s and '60s. They had a blast. In those days you could bring coolers into the games, and it wasn't unusual to see fans carry in jugs of mixed drinks. The tailgating never stopped, moving from the parking lots right into the stadium.

This was still a time when going to a game was like going to a nice party. Women wore dresses, and the men, sporting ties, usually supplied an orange and blue corsage for their dates. Crowds were introduced to night football during this era, the first being played against The Citadel on September 23, 1950.

Florida Field had three expansions during these two decades. The first one, which began in 1949 and was com-pleted for the 1950 season, increased capacity to 40,116. But because Florida was still struggling to find consistent success, fans who bought tickets could sit almost anywhere they wanted.

During this period, Otis Boggs became a major part of the game day experience. Boggs was the Florida radio play-by-play man starting in 1940 and soon became the voice of Florida football. Fans would bring transistor radios to the games and listen to his broadcasts. He also hosted a Monday night highlights radio show.

Florida football took on an air of excitement in the early 1960s with the arrival of coach Ray Graves and quarter-back Larry Libertore, and the fans responded by filling up the stands. Another expansion, this time on the east side, took the capacity to 56,164. And for Steve Spurrier's senior year, bleachers were added to the south end zone to raise the capacity to 62,800.

Florida Field kept getting bigger and bigger to adapt to the growing interest in the Gators. By 1966, Steve Spurrier's senior season, bleachers had been added to take the capacity up to more than 62,000.

No Bowl for You

Although the Gators finished with a solid record in 1957 that included this 14–7 win over Vanderbilt, the team would not be invited to a bowl game due to violations involving UF's basketball and baseball recruits.

Florida's 1957 football team was good enough on the field to make a bowl game. But something that happened off the field kept the Gators home for the holidays.

"It had to do with bringing a baseball player and a basketball player to campus for a recruiting trip," said Jimmy Dunn, quarterback of the 1957 team. "It was one of those deals where everybody was doing it but the NCAA came down on Florida. There was nothing we could do about it. But we were 18-, 19-, 20-year-old kids. We didn't know what to expect. We just went out and played football."

Fans who had become disgruntled with Bob Woodruff's conservative play calling were softening after big wins in 1956 over Louisiana State, Auburn, and Georgia on consecutive Saturdays by a combined score of 69–6. Woodruff's defense was stout and limited opponents to 98 total points that year. The 1956 team went 6–3–1, and big things were expected the following year with most of the team coming back.

Dunn, a smallish 140-pound quarterback from Tampa, provided a spark in 1957, and Bernie Parrish was an outstanding two-way player for the team. The Gators finished 6–2–1, the nine-game season coming about when the Asian flu hit the Florida team and forced the cancellation of the opener against UCLA.

Despite the solid record, there would be no bowl game for the 1957 team. The NCAA had placed the Gators on probation for the whole season. The infractions weren't football related but instead involved the transportation and feeding of basketball and baseball recruits. Still, the sanctions meant a one-year bowl ban for the football team.

The Gators went out and had an excellent season anyway. They stunned 10th-ranked LSU and its Heisman winner Billy Cannon 22–14 on October 26 and handled Vanderbilt 14–7 on November 16. Parrish scored both touchdowns, kicked both extra points, and was named National Back of the Week.

"It was just one of those games," Parrish said. "I led the team in tackles too."

The only two losses came at homecoming against Mississippi State 29–20 and at fourth-ranked Auburn 13–0. The tie was disappointing when neither Florida nor Georgia Tech could muster any points. Florida did score on a pass from Parrish to Jim Rountree, but a penalty wiped out the play.

The Gators finished the successful season by winning at Miami 14–0, ending a four-game losing streak against the Hurricanes on November 30. The Gators ended their season earlier than they would have liked, finishing with a ranking of 20th in the Associated Press poll.

Close to Great in '58

By 1958, it was time for Florida to start playing rival Florida State. The Gators won the first game 21–7 behind quarterback Jimmy Dunn, and one of the fiercest rivalries in college football was born.

Before the arrival of Steve Spurrier as coach in 1990, Florida football was known for what almost was. The 1958 team falls into that category.

Florida's team in '58 was geared for defense, and it showed all season. The Gators knocked off UCLA 21–14 in the third game of the season and came within a hair of beating eventual national champion LSU before losing 10–7. Against defending national champion Auburn, Florida appeared headed for an upset win.

Down 6–3, the Gators drove to the Auburn 3 before losing the ball on a fumble. After the Tigers took a safety on fourth down, Florida again drove deep into Auburn territory, but Joe Hergert missed a game-winning field goal as UF lost 6–5.

By 1958, there was a new rival for the Gators. Florida State, which had previously been an all-women's school, had been pushing since 1951 to start a series with Florida. In 1958, the Seminoles got their wish.

On November 22 at Florida Field, the rivalry that is now one of the most heated in college football was born. Jimmy Dunn, who had been told by FSU coach Tom Nugent that he lacked the "moral fiber" necessary to play for him, was named the Most Valuable Player in the game. He made a touchdown-saving tackle on the opening kickoff, then ran for two scores as Florida won 21–7. Dave Hudson scored the other touchdown on a blocked punt. This time, the Gators wouldn't be denied a bowl berth.

Back to the Gator

For the second time in the school's history, Florida would play in a bowl game in 1958. And for the second time, it would be the Gator Bowl in Jacksonville.

On December 27, 1958, the Gators took on SEC rival Mississippi in the first UF game to be televised. The result was a 7–3 loss that was difficult to accept.

Ole Miss scored on its first possession, but Jimmy Dunn drove the Gators back down the field for a field goal. Trailing 7–3, Florida would drive deep into Ole Miss territory three times. But fumbles ended two drives, and the third was stopped on a down at the Rebels' 3-yard line.

Florida outgained Mississippi 215 yards to 184 but couldn't put the winning score in the end zone. In many ways, it was emblematic of the Woodruff era—close but no cigar.

Ray Graves: The Bull Gator

After Bob Woodruff was let go, Florida turned to another former Tennessee player to become its next head coach. With a starting salary of $19,000 a year, Ray Graves was hired to bring some life to the program. He was not the first choice, but Florida had botched a chance to get Ara Parseghian away from Northwestern by wasting time on Delaware's Davey Nelson (who turned down UF). Florida president Dr. Wayne Reitz then called Georgia Tech coach Bobby Dodd, who recommended Graves, one of his assistants.

Where Woodruff had been distant and at times abrasive with boosters, Graves came in with an outgoing, down-home personality and a desire to make everyone happy. Florida fans had no idea what they were about to experience. Although Graves never won the SEC, he finished second three times. During Graves's ten seasons, the Gators, who had been to two bowl games in their history, went to five and their first-ever major bowl, the Sugar Bowl. Florida also had its first Heisman Trophy winner in Steve Spurrier, and 12 times Florida players were honored as first-team All-Americans.

These were giddy times for the Gators, but it wasn't all good. It was in the 1960s that "Wait 'Til Next Year" gained momentum as a slogan to describe Florida football—and not in a good way. Graves won 69 percent of his games as the UF coach, but that seemed to make the losses that

much more heartbreaking, including the first-ever loss to Florida State 16–7 in 1964.

Because of Graves's early success, expectations rose with each season. Only his second team failed to produce a winning record, and seven-win seasons became the norm. Three times—in 1960, 1966, and 1969—Florida won nine games.

Although Graves was a defense-first coach, he was able to adapt to the personnel he recruited. When he brought Spurrier into the fold, he went to a more pro-style passing game.

When Ray Graves arrived, it represented a new era at UF. Graves, posing here with his assistants in 1962, had three nine-win seasons during his tenure and led the Gators to their first ever major bowl game.

When Florida faced Tennessee in the 1969 Gator Bowl, few knew it would be Ray Graves's last game and that the opposing coach, Doug Dickey, would be taking over at Florida. John Reaves (7) led Florida to a 14–13 victory.

After Spurrier left, the Gators were more of an option team with quarterbacks Larry Rentz and Jackie Eckdahl. And when strong-armed John Reaves became the quarterback in 1969, it was bombs away.

Florida had some of its brightest moments to date under Graves. The 1960 upset of Georgia Tech, the 1962 Gator Bowl win over ninth-ranked Penn State, the stunning win over No. 3 Alabama in Tuscaloosa in 1963, and the come-from-behind win over Georgia in 1967 were among them.

Graves's 1968 team was supposed to be one of his best. But an injury to All-America tailback Larry Smith derailed the season, and Florida went 6–3–1. Most embarrassing was a rain-soaked 51–0 loss to Georgia when Graves decided

to switch his offensive and defensive coordinators for the week. The boosters became restless, and a mutual decision

One of the biggest accomplishments in Ray Graves's ten seasons at Florida was convincing a quarterback from Johnson City, Tennessee, to play for UF. Steve Spurrier went on to leave an indelible mark on the program.

was reached that Graves would step down after the 1969 season.

Graves responded with a 9–1–1 season that culminated with a win over Tennessee in the Gator Bowl. Before the game, Florida had already made the decision to hire Tennessee coach Doug Dickey. Graves's last great season had come too late.

Graves, whose 70 wins were the most by a Florida coach until they were surpassed by Spurrier, remained at Florida as athletic director until 1980.

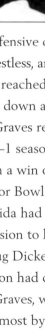

Injury-Laden Florida Leaves For Kentucky

Four Players Left Behind, Two Taken In Doubtful Status

GAINESVILLE — (AP) — A 41-man University of Florida football squad left by plane this morning for Lexington where it will meet the Kentucky Wildcats, leaders of the Southeastern conference, Saturday afternoon.

Left behind were varsity regulars who are still recuperating from injuries that have plagued the Gators during the past two weeks.

Loren Broadus, senior halfback and alternate captain, did not board the plane at the local airport. Neither did Mack Gilstrap, ace line-backer and Jimmy Rawls, defensive guard.

Jack Nichols, sophomore halfback, had a leg injury that kept him behind. Guard Dickie Rowe and tackle Charles Lapradd, who have been sidelines, made the trip, however.

Coach Bob Woodruff himself was limping slightly from a wrenched knee he suffered demonstrating a play to his offensive platoon in Thursday afternoon's drill. Only the linemen saw contact action in a workout of their own yesterday. Backs and ends worked on aerial offense and defense, weapons on which the Gators are expected to rely heavily.

The relatively light drill climaxed a week's ban on scrimmage sessions that might have added new names to the casualty list.

"We'll probably have some more injuries Saturday," Woodruff said wearily.

"We'll be fielding a comparatively small team."

Florida has played in the Gator Bowl more than any other bowl game. The first was in 1953 and the last in 1992. The Gators have played in eight contests and won six of them.

The 1950 Gator team was 5–1 and ranked 17th in the nation when they traveled to Lexington, Kentucky, to face the No. 5 Wildcats. Kentucky was too good for the injury-depleted Gators, winning 40–6.

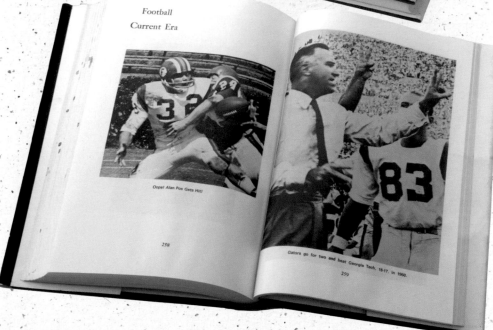

The history of Florida football has been well chronicled because of the huge fan base that spreads throughout the country. Arthur Cobb's book takes fans through the Steve Spurrier years.

This ticket stub is from Florida's first-ever bowl game. On January 1, 1953, the Gators traveled to Jacksonville to face Tulsa in the Gator Bowl and came away with a 14–13 win, thanks to a missed extra point by Tulsa in the fourth quarter.

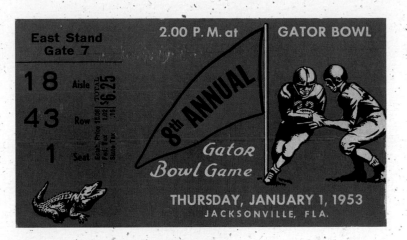

This Gator figurine includes an interesting helmet and a Gator with a toothy growl. Florida fans can't get their hands on enough UF memorabilia, whether it's in local shops or online.

Georgia vs Florida
November 9, 1957

Price 50c

This guide is a great example of UF's plan to wipe out each team it encountered. Florida blasted the Georgia Bulldogs 22–0 during the 1957 meeting of the SEC rivals.

It's not often that orange and blue go together, but they do when a Gator fan is dressing for a game. An orange and blue tie is the perfect accessory to a day at The Swamp.

Graves Starts with a Bang

Ray Graves began his UF coaching career on the right foot, to say the least. The Gators went 9–2, including a 13–12 win over Baylor in the Gator Bowl. The only SEC loss in 1960 for that team came against 14th-ranked Auburn.

Ray Graves wasted little time showing that things were going to be different at Florida. In his first season, the Gators went 9–2 and had a program-defining win in Graves's third game as coach.

On October 1, 1960, the Gators played host to tenth-ranked Georgia Tech, which was coached by the same Bobby Dodd who had recommended Graves for the Florida job. To add to the drama, Dodd's son Bobby Jr. was one of the Florida quarterbacks. Bobby Jr. was the passer, while Larry Libertore was the running quarterback.

In a game where third-down punts were still in vogue, Florida trailed 17–10 late in the game before embarking on an 85-yard touchdown drive. Florida moved the ball to the 1-yard line, where Bobby Jr. fumbled the snap, setting up a fourth-down play at the 4.

Libertore came in and rolled right before making a late pitch to halfback Lindy Infante. Infante snuck into the corner of the end zone with 33 seconds to play. What followed was a play that would make Graves instantly famous, in part because of the picture of him signaling for a two-point conversion on the sidelines.

With the crowd screaming for Florida to go for the win, Graves went for two, and Libertore found halfback Jon Macbeth in the end zone. Macbeth made a juggling catch for the 18–17 victory.

Although the Gators followed that with a loss to Rice in Miami, they would lose only once in SEC play that season—to Auburn 10–7. The record was good enough for a Gator Bowl berth, where they handled Baylor 13–12 in front of 50,122 in Jacksonville when the Bears failed to convert a late two-point conversion. The Graves era was off to a flying start.

He didn't know it at the time, but this would be the most famous picture of Ray Graves. He signaled for a two-point conversion in the last seconds of the game at Georgia Tech, and the Gators converted, winning 18–17 in an emotionally charged game.

Beating 'Bama

As Florida's success began to escalate, so did the enthusiasm of the student body. Pep rallies were held prior to games, and big wins on the road meant thousands of fans would show up to greet the team at the airport.

Sometimes a big bowl win can bleed into the following season. Players are inspired by their success and work harder in the off-season. They enter the next season with determination to repeat that success with the carrot of another bowl trip dangling in the distance.

But early in the 1963 season—despite coming off a big Gator Bowl win over Penn State—it didn't look that way for the Gators. They lost to Georgia Tech in Atlanta 9–0, tied Mississippi State 9–9, and were unimpressive in holding off Richmond 35–28.

Next up: No. 3 Alabama.

Although Florida had won in Tuscaloosa before, the Gators had never beaten legendary coach Paul "Bear" Bryant there. Then, it was called Denny Stadium, but it would later be named Bryant-Denny Stadium in honor of the most successful coach in SEC history.

Few gave Florida a chance because of the Gators' slow start and the power of the Crimson Tide and their quarterback Joe Namath. But somehow, it happened.

Florida stifled Namath, who was already dealing with knee issues that would plague him throughout his career. Bobby Lyle kicked an early field goal, and the Gator defense was making it stand up. Suddenly, it was 10–0. Halfback Dick Kirk burst through the line and was untouched on a 40-yard touchdown run early in the fourth quarter. Although Kirk wasn't known for his speed, he looked like a bullet shooting through the Tide defense.

Namath scored late in the game, but the Gators left town with a 10–6 victory on October 12.

The Celebration

When Florida teams recorded a big victory on the road, it wasn't unusual for Gator fans who had listened to the game on college radio station WRUF to head to the airport and greet the team.

But no Gator team had seen anything like this.

When the team got off the plane after the 10–6 win over Alabama, there were 10,000 fans mobbing the tiny Gainesville airport waiting to greet them. The line of fans extended along the road where cars had found makeshift parking places to cheer for the boys who had done the unthinkable. And along Waldo Road, which leads to the airport, there were even more fans applauding the buses as they took the team back to campus.

Sending Out an S.O.S.

It was a beautiful day in Gainesville, and Ray Graves had a prize recruit in town who liked to play golf. Since the school had just purchased the Gainesville Country Club near campus, Graves took his recruit to the course to hit the driving range.

The outing would ultimately change the course of University of Florida football.

Ray Graves found out about Stephen Orr Spurrier through Graves's brother Edwin, who lived in Knoxville, Tennessee. He encouraged the Florida coach to recruit the player from Johnson City, Tennessee, who could do it all—throw, run, kick, punt...and win.

Despite suffering from the flu during his visit to Gainesville, Spurrier liked what he saw on campus. The weather, the golf courses, the offense—he was impressed. Spurrier decided to be a Gator, and nobody could have possibly known what an impact it would have. Graves used a ploy that Spurrier would later use in recruiting when he became Florida head coach in 1990: If everyone wants to live in Florida when they're finished playing, why not move to the Sunshine State when you're a young man?

Spurrier and Tommy Shannon shared quarterback duties in 1964, the year Spurrier was named SEC sophomore of the year. But over the next two seasons Spurrier would rewrite the Florida record books and change Florida football history.

In his junior and senior seasons, Spurrier threw for 3,905 yards and 30 touchdowns. He led Florida to its first two major bowl appearances. And in 1966, he would win Florida's first-ever Heisman Trophy.

Spurrier, who would be named to the College Football Hall of Fame in 1986, broke every school and SEC passing record during his three seasons at UF. And he engineered some of the greatest comebacks in Gator history. He had a confidence in the huddle that bordered on cockiness—plus the ability to back it up.

When he easily won the Heisman in 1966 over Purdue's Bob Griese, Spurrier took the advice of Jacksonville TV personality Dick Stratton. He accepted the trophy, then called UF president J. Wayne Reitz to the podium

Steve Spurrier liked everything about Gainesville when he made his official visit. That included an offense that would be suited to his strengths. It paid off when he won the Heisman Trophy in 1966.

Ray Graves was a father figure to the boys he coached—especially to Steve Spurrier, who often called his own plays in the huddle and sometimes drew them up in the dirt.

to take the trophy for the school. It was typical Spurrier and changed the way the Downtown Athletic Club gave out college football's most prestigious award. From then on, the player and his school each received a trophy (Spurrier received his own trophy later).

The culmination of Spurrier's career came in the Orange Bowl on January 2, 1967. The unranked Gators were coming off a disappointing loss to Miami to close out the regular season, and Georgia Tech was ranked eighth in the country. But Spurrier's passing and the running of Larry Smith, who had 187 rushing yards and a 94-yard touchdown run, were too much for the Yellow Jackets. Florida won 27–12, a fitting end to the career of a quarterback who went 23–9 during his time at Florida.

In 2006, Spurrier was one of four players inducted into UF's new Ring of Honor, which celebrates the greatest players in Gator history.

The Comebacks

It didn't take long for Steve Spurrier to make an impact on Florida's football program. In his second game as a Gator, Florida trailed 13–10 with three minutes to go. But Spurrier engineered a pair of drives that resulted in field goals and a 16–13 win. And the hits kept coming.

- Trailing 10–7 with four minutes to play against Georgia in 1965, Spurrier drove the Gators 77 yards for the winning score, a 19-yard pass to halfback Jack Harper.

- Trailing 17–16 against Florida State in 1965 with two minutes to go, Spurrier drove Florida 71 yards for the winning score.

- Trailing Florida State 19–14 in 1966, Spurrier hit Larry Smith with the winning touchdown pass and converted a two-point conversion to give UF a 22–19 win.

In all, Spurrier led Florida to eight wins during his career when the Gators were trailing or tied heading into the fourth quarter.

No matter the situation, Florida's players were always confident that Steve Spurrier would find a way to rally the team to a victory. Here, he attempts to throw a pass amidst intense pressure from Georgia.

It's What's in You

Dr. Robert Cade's "thirst quencher" was a mixture of sodium and glucose that helped Florida players in the heat of the Sunshine State. As the late Dr. Cade said during a national commercial, "Naturally, we called it Gatorade."

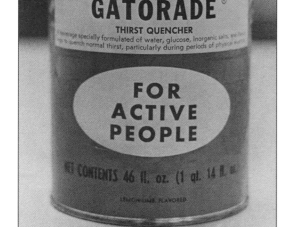

Dr. Robert Cade came to Florida in 1961 and became the school's first kidney specialist. But his impact on the world of sports began in 1965 when Cade and fellow researchers decided to invent a drink that would help the football team perform better in the fourth quarter.

Dr. Cade and his team came up with a mixture of glucose and sodium and tried it out on the freshmen team. Players complained that it tasted like, well, a yellow bodily fluid. Determined to conduct his research to the fullest, Dr. Cade went as far as to taste the bodily fluid for comparison. He must have agreed with the players' assessment, because he began squeezing lemons into the mixture to make the taste more tolerable.

When Florida went 9–2 in 1966, the mixture—named Gatorade—was given a good part of the credit. Dr. Cade offered to sell the rights to the university, but when the school balked he sold them to food manufacturer Stokely Van Camp. Eventually, an agreement was worked out between Dr. Cade and the university to share the rights to Gatorade.

The drink became a worldwide sensation (it's now sold in 80 countries), and the university has received more than $100 mil-

With Gatorade a success, Dr. Robert Cade moved on to new ventures, including Gator Go!, a high-protein drink. Here, All-America running back Larry Smith samples a carton.

lion in royalties over the years. Dr. Cade donated a portion of his royalties to fund scholarships and endow a chair at the UF medical school.

Dr. Cade died on November 27, 2007, at the age of 80. He enjoyed a revival late in his life when Gatorade featured him in its line of commercials with college football announcer Keith Jackson. His other inventions—a high-protein milk drink called Gator Go! and the alcoholic beverage Hop 'N' Gator—didn't catch on. But with Gatorade, his legend continues.

Go for Two

Florida received a bid to play in its first major bowl with two games remaining in the 1965 season. The team would travel to New Orleans for a New Year's Day Sugar Bowl encounter with Missouri. The good news was that Steve Spurrier was named the game's Most Valuable Player. The bad news was that it didn't matter.

After accepting the bid, Florida lost to Miami but pulled out a come-from-behind win over Florida State. But in New Orleans, the Gators couldn't get it going. They fell behind 17–0 at the half and 20–0 with just over ten minutes to play in the game. Then suddenly, Spurrier caught fire.

Moving on Up

Following the 1965 season, demand for tickets had risen to the point where Florida Field needed another expansion. The football program also needed an upgrade in several other areas.

Seating began to build up the east side of the stadium, and the new construction would also include a dormitory for the athletes, a new onsite training table, and a new, much-needed weight room. The 10,000-seat expansion would raise the capacity to 56,164, and bleachers were also added to the south end zone to take that capacity to 62,800 a year later.

The athletic dorms would be named Yon Hall after Everett Yon, a former player and coach and a prominent Gator booster.

Spurrier began changing formations and made up some plays on his own. He drove Florida for a touchdown, hitting Jack Harper from 22 yards out. But Florida's coaches inexplicably decided to go for two. Later, offensive coordinator Ed Kensler said he thought 20–8 would look better than 20–7.

Spurrier wasn't finished, driving the Gators to two more scores in the waning minutes. Again, Florida went for two after each touchdown and failed to convert. The final was a painful 20–18.

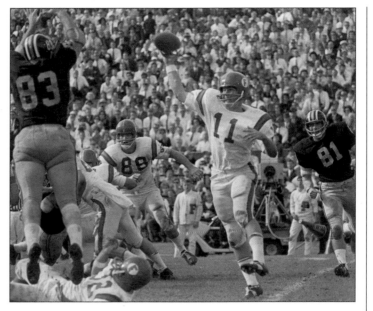

Steve Spurrier (11) set records for passing in the 1966 Sugar Bowl, but it wasn't enough. He rallied the Gators from a 20–0 fourth-quarter deficit, but three attempts to convert two-point plays failed, and UF lost 20–18.

Spurrier finished the game with 352 passing yards, two touchdowns passing, and one touchdown rushing. But it just wasn't enough.

Florida Field was packed for games as Florida began to find a place on the college football map. Expansion of the stadium included Yon Hall, a dormitory for athletes.

The Kick

On October 29, 1966, the eyes of the college football world were on Florida's homecoming game against Auburn. Sportswriters descended on Gainesville from all over the country to see if this Steve Spurrier character was for real. He gave them quite a show, and any who weren't there were briefed in the next few days by Florida sports information director Norm Carlson.

Florida dominated the game, but Auburn found other ways besides offense to score. Larry Ellis ran a kickoff back 89 yards for one score, and Gusty Yearout plucked a Tommy Christian fumble off the back of a Gator lineman and ran it 91 yards for a score with Spurrier and wide receiver Richard Trapp in hot pursuit.

Despite Florida having a huge statistical edge, the score was tied at 27 with four minutes to go when Florida got the ball. With Spurrier calling his own plays, the Gators drove down the field. But an intentional grounding call on Spurrier backed the Gators up to the Auburn 40. On third down, Spurrier hit Jack Coons on a delay pattern. Fourth down. The 40-yard kick would be right at the edge of the range of kicker Wayne "Shadetree" Barfield.

Spurrier approached coach Graves. "Let me kick it," he said. Spurrier had kicked a couple of field goals in Florida's opener that season against Northwestern but had tried only one other during the season. Some of the UF coaches urged Graves to let Barfield try it. But Graves was a big believer that Spurrier could do anything.

Spurrier put on his square-toed shoe and boomed the 40-yarder into history. Convinced that it must be a fake, Auburn's players barely rushed the kick. The kick not only won the game 30–27 for Florida but probably won the Heisman Trophy for Spurrier.

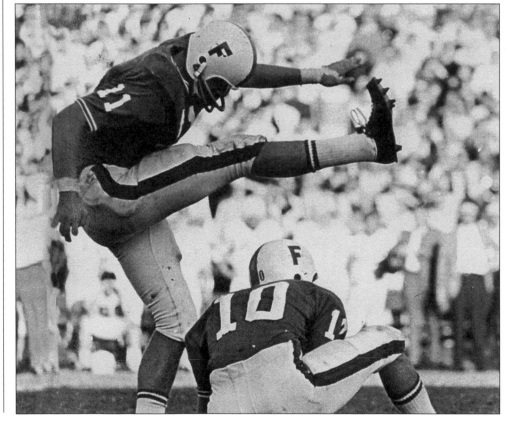

If there was one play that won the Heisman Trophy for Steve Spurrier, it was his 40-yard field goal that beat Auburn 30–27 in 1966. Spurrier wasn't Florida's regular kicker but insisted on trying it because it was out of the range of Wayne Barfield.

Super Sophs

The last season for Ray Graves as coach of the Florida Gators was one of the best in school history. A group of veterans was injected with life from a group of sophomores who made Florida one of the most exciting teams in the country. The "Super Sophs" were quarterback John Reaves, receiver Carlos Alvarez, fullback Mike Rich, and tailback Tommy Durrance, who would set the school record that season for touchdowns.

It started early. On the third play of the season against heavily favored Houston, a team that had been picked No. 1 by *Playboy* magazine, Reaves hit Alvarez streaking down the east sideline for a 70-yard touchdown. The Gators went on to win 59–34, and fans who had been listening to the game on the radio started showing up at halftime to buy tickets.

Florida continued its roll through the schedule. The Gators were 6–0 and ranked seventh before they went to Auburn, where Reaves set an NCAA record that still stands—nine interceptions in a game. The 38–12 loss was followed by a disappointing tie against Georgia when the Gators missed a late field goal.

A strong finish included Alvarez catching 15 passes in a 35–16 win in Miami and a 9–1–1 overall record after a bowl win over Tennessee.

Despite the disappointment of 1968, Florida coaches knew they had something special on the horizon—a group of sophomores that included tailback Tommy Durrance (20). They would become known as the "Super Sophs."

John Reaves may have been riding an alligator in this picture, but Florida rode his right arm during the 1969 season. The young star teamed up with fellow sophomore Carlos Alvarez to form one of the nation's best passing tandems.

Bold Finish

It was just weird. Florida finished the 1969 campaign against fellow SEC team Tennessee in the Gator Bowl. Nobody wrote about the impending game because rumors were flying that Ray Graves was out and Doug Dickey, the Tennessee coach and former UF quarterback, was going to be the next coach.

Reporters kept going back and forth between the two training camps in Jacksonville and Daytona Beach, trying to get the scoop. Graves had second thoughts about leaving before deciding to resign two days before the game.

Finally, a game was played on December 27 in Jacksonville. The Gators got one score on a blocked punt returned for a touchdown by Mike Kelley. The game-winner came on a pass from John Reaves to Carlos Alvarez. The 14–13 final allowed Graves to go out with a victory and set the stage for more drama.

All-Everything

During the winning eras of Bob Woodruff and Ray Graves, Florida had more stars on the football field than ever before. The university had only two first-team All-America players in its history before Woodruff's arrival. He had three alone during his ten years as UF's coach.

Charlie LaPradd, a rugged tackle, played both ways for UF's first bowl team and was named an All-American in 1952. John Barrow was a guard who was an All-American in 1956 and went on to a distinguished career in the Canadian Football League. Vel Heckman played tackle for Woodruff and was one of the quickest at his position in the country, making the All-America team in 1958.

Under Graves, the honors came in waves. Larry Dupree rushed for 1,725 yards in his career and was honored in 1964. He was followed the next year by tough defensive end Lynn Matthews, nifty safety Bruce Bennett, wide receiver Charlie Casey, physical guard Larry Gagner, and quarterback Steve Spurrier.

Spurrier and his center Bill Carr, who started 32 consecutive games, were honored in 1966. In 1968 tailback Larry Smith overcame a season full of injuries and was joined as an All-American by guard Guy Dennis, who went on to a seven-year NFL career. In the last year of his career, Graves saw receiver Carlos Alvarez and cornerback Steve Tannen honored.

Indeed, these were heady times for the football program. Woodruff had laid the foundation, and Graves had Florida finally gaining consistent national attention. Even today, some of the stars of these eras remain the favorites of old-time Gators.

The players from the Graves era still meet annually at a "Silver Sixties" reunion where the same stories are told and retold.

Despite a pair of injuries during his senior year, Larry Smith was healthy enough to be named All-American and finished his career with a touchdown run in the 1968 Miami game.

Forward Progress

College football began to slowly integrate in the 1950s after the Supreme Court's mandate in 1954. But it was even slower to have an impact in the South. The first African American to play in an SEC game wasn't until 1967 when Nat Northington hit the field for Kentucky in a game against Ole Miss. The following year, Florida got in on the act.

On December 17, 1968, at his home in Tampa, Leonard George became the first black player to sign a football scholarship with the University of Florida. A day later, Willie Jackson from Sarasota became the second.

George would make more history on September 26, 1970. The sophomore tailback became the first African American to score a touchdown in Alabama's Denny Stadium. The Tide was still two years away from integrating Bear Bryant's team.

George played that 1970 season at tailback but switched to defensive back for his last two seasons. Jackson caught 75 passes, eight of them for touchdowns, and was the Gators' main kickoff returner.

These were troubled times at Florida, which still only had 343 African American students by the time George and Jackson were seniors. A protest on campus by the Black Student Union in April 1971 resulted in dozens of arrests. Jackson served as spokesperson for the ten black

athletes on campus and said they would remain at school and try to make things work.

By then, fullback Vince Kendrick and tailback Lenny Lucas had joined George and Jackson as African American players for UF. By 1973, one-third of the Florida roster would be black.

Jackson had two sons who played significant roles on future Gator teams. Willie was an All-SEC receiver who played from 1991 to '93. Terry was a halfback from 1995 to '98 who scored the clinching touchdown in Florida's national championship win in the 1997 Sugar Bowl.

Willie Jackson, one of the first black players to sign with Florida, saw two of his sons play for the Gators, including Terry (22). He was one of the heroes of Florida's first-ever national title win against Florida State in New Orleans.

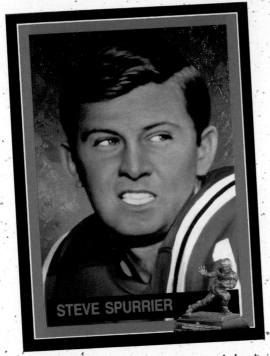

The 1966 Heisman Trophy recipient was Florida's Steve Spurrier. That honor also landed the UF quarterback in a set of trading cards that featured past winners.

J ♣

Jack Youngblood
Defensive End, 1968-1970

Set the standard to which Gator defensive linemen are measured; 1970 All-American

After excelling in Florida's football program, Jack Youngblood went on to dominate in the NFL, playing 14 seasons with the Los Angeles Rams.

Gater Growl

THE PEOPLES CHOICE

GATORPOLL
"Gators Reign in '68 Campaign!"

ADEMY -vs- FLORIDA
M · TAMPA, FLORIDA
, 1968 - 2:00 P. M.
OR ADMISSION
T SEAT ASSIGNMENT
STAND
T HAVE TICKETS
ESS OF AGE

There were high hopes for Florida's 1968 season, and it started in Tampa. There, the sixth-ranked Gators opened the season with a 23–20 win over Air Force on September 21.

The theme for the 1968 Gator Growl the night before the homecoming game against Auburn was the presidential campaign. The Growl is the nation's largest student-run pep rally.

Gators Have Shoes To Fill

HINTON   McCALL

GAINESVILLE — There are big shoes to fill, and little ones, too, at center and linebacker for Florida this fall.

Big ones belong to all-American and captain Bill Carr, the 6-4 ace who started 32 straight games for the Gators before graduating and going on to the New Orleans Saints.

Little ones were worn by No. 1, wee Jack Card, a tough and dedicated linebacker for three years. With Card went Florida's two other linebackers of note, Steve Heidt and Charlie Pippin.

Defensive captain Wayne McCall, a versatile player out of Ocala, moves into linebacker this fall after last year's positions of safety, linebacker and end. He will be helped by oft-hurt Chip Hinton, a stout and steady boy from Pensacola who can mingle with the best of them when healthy, and junior college transfer David Mann, also of Pensacola.

"We hope to get sound linebacking out of these three," says head coach Ray Graves. "Some youngsters might be able to help, boys like Mike Palahach and Wayne Compton, but this would be a bonus."

Graves is most concerned about his linebacking situation.

Three boys are attempting to replace Carr at center. Heading the list at present is sophomore Kim Helton, who starts the fall on the springboard of an excellent spring's practice, are sophomore Nick Sinardi of Tampa and junior Dave Burnhart of West Palm Beach.

"This could be a real good fight," says Graves. "Right now, based on spring practice, Helton's the boy but the other two have the potential to unseat him."

Gator Ducat Interest Higher

GAINESVILLE—Interest in University of Florida football, as exhibited by the number of tickets sold, has never been higher.

Director of Athletics Ray Graves reported that the Gators final total sale on season tickets reached 20,000, over 5,000 more than in any previous season, and that the FSU game on November 25 is a complete sellout.

Only 6,500 end zone tickets remain for the Georgia game, set for November 11 in the newly-enlarged 68,000 capacity) Gator Bowl in Jacksonville. Stadium capacity at Florida Field has also been increased by additions to both end zones and the Gator home playing field can now hold almost 60,000 fans.

"This is tremendous response and support," Graves notes.

"We are already assured of a record year in attendance at home."

After a pair of wins to start the season, Florida lost at home against Louisiana State University 37–6 in 1967. The LSU series has been a permanent part of the UF schedule since 1971.

In 1967, the season after Steve Spurrier won the Heisman Trophy, Florida had to replace a large group of stars. A stunning win over Georgia 17–16 was the highlight of a 6–4 season.

A♦

John Reaves
Quarterback, 1969-1971

Strong armed passer left Florida as the NCAA's all-time leading passer with 7,581 yards; 1971 All-American

The Gators finished 9–1–1 in 1969 during John Reaves's sophomore year at quarterback.

Pins were a big part of the Game Day experience starting in the 1950s. Today, most of the pins worn by Gator fans are simply asking their team to "Beat" the next team on the schedule.

Florida's powerful and entertaining 1969 team continued its undefeated season with a 41–20 win over Vanderbilt. The win put UF at 6–0 and earned the Gators a ranking of No. 7 in the country.

THE ROLLER COASTER RIDE

1970–1989

It was wild. Crazy. Bizarre. In the 1970s and '80s, Florida football would be a huge story not only in the state but across the nation. Sometimes for the right reasons; sometimes for the wrong ones. During these two decades, two coaches were fired because of NCAA violations. But there were also some amazing wins during this time and some of the greatest Gator players to ever grace the field.

The face of Florida football would change in the 1970s with the introduction of integration to the football team. Players such as Lenny Lucas (right) began to be a part of the Gator Nation.

There was no shortage of star players at Florida during the 1970s and 1980s—and none of them was bigger than Emmitt Smith. Smith wasted little time making an impact on the SEC and the national stage.

Dickey Comes Home

Doug Dickey was raised in Gainesville and was a quarterback at Florida from 1951 to '53. So when he returned to the school as head coach in 1970, you would think he would have been welcomed with open arms.

But the players on the Gator team, who were coming off a 9–1–1 season, felt betrayed. Coach Ray Graves, who had been like a father to many of the players, had decided before the 1969 season that it would be his last. Star receiver Carlos Alvarez led the revolt, eventually forming a group called the League of Athletes, which demanded players' rights.

"I felt like I had been betrayed," Alvarez said. "Most of the players would have told you the same thing. I was just more vocal. The blame was never on Coach Dickey. I was mad at the school president, Stephen O'Connell. We were told before the Gator Bowl game [in 1969] by O'Connell that nothing was going to happen.

"I was totally committed to Coach Dickey," Alvarez continued. "But his style was so different [than Graves's]. He had a coaching style that didn't fit the players he had."

Dickey believed in taking few chances and running the ball with the option. But he had a pro-style quarterback in John Reaves. The result his first year in 1970 was a disappointing 7–4 record. Dickey's mantra of "you have to avoid losing and then win the game" didn't sit well with the Florida faithful.

The following year, Florida was 4–7. There was one shining moment in 1971 when 0–5 Florida stunned 5–0 Florida State on October 16 by a score of 17–15.

By 1973, Florida seemed poised for a run at the SEC crown. But an injury to Nat Moore, the team's top running back, derailed those hopes, and Florida was 2–4 when Dickey made the decision to give Don Gaffney a start at Auburn. Gaffney became the first African American

Florida went to the wishbone offense in the mid-1970s, and that became the "whoosh-bone" when the backfield included speedy quarterback Terry LeCount (7) along with Earl Carr (30), Tony Green (33), and Willie Wilder (44) in 1977.

He had been a Florida quarterback, but the arrival of Doug Dickey as Florida's new coach was not without controversy. Many players felt betrayed by the departure of coach Ray Graves.

to play the position at UF, and the Gators won for the first time in Jordan-Hare Stadium 12–8.

"Coach Dickey walked up to me in the locker room before the game and handed me a football," Gaffney said. "He said, 'Don, you got it.' You could hear a pin drop."

The next two seasons saw Dickey go to the wishbone attack with a stellar group of running backs like Tony Green and Jimmy DuBose and with Gaffney at the controls. The Gators went to the Sugar Bowl following the 1974 season but lost to Nebraska 13–10, due in part to a goal-line stand by the Cornhuskers.

Florida needed only to beat Georgia in 1975 to win the SEC, but Dickey's conservative play calling doomed Florida 10–7. That team lost two games by a total of four points but ended up going to the Gator Bowl. On a rainy night, the Gators seemed uninspired in a 13–0 loss.

Again in 1976, Dickey had a powerhouse team, but a decision to go for a fourth-and-one at their own 29 backfired. Georgia stuffed Earl Carr and went on to a 41–27 win.

After a 6–4–1 season in 1977, Dickey's job was on the line. His team responded by going 4–7. Sometimes cold to his players and always battling with the press, Dickey was let go before the final game of the season, a 22–21 loss to Miami. On the artificial turf at Florida Field, an angry fan had burned "Dump Dickey" into the playing surface prior to the game. It was hardly the way a coach who had come so close to winning Florida's first SEC title wanted to go out.

One thing Doug Dickey was able to do was handle FSU. Dickey's Florida teams won the first seven games against the Gators' arch rival, including this 33–26 victory in 1976.

"Fourth-and-Dumb"

Doug Dickey's teams in 1975 and '76 were among the best to ever suit up for the Gators. One thing stood in the way of an SEC crown each year, however: Georgia.

Florida went into the 1975 game unbeaten in conference play and ranked 11th in the nation. Georgia was not ranked, but Bulldogs' coach Vince Dooley had something up his sleeve.

With Florida leading 7–3 and only 3:24 to play, that first SEC title looked within reach. But Georgia tight end Richard Appleby took a handoff on what looked to be a reverse that the Bulldogs had run earlier in the season. Instead, he stopped and launched a perfect pass to a streaking Gene Washington down the east sideline for an 80-yard score and a 10–7 victory.

A year later, Florida's attack was working brilliantly, and the Gators led 27–13 at the half. But Georgia scored to cut into the lead, and Florida was faced with a fourth down at its own 29. Dickey didn't want to let the Bulldogs keep the momentum and went for it, but Earl Carr, a 220-pound tailback, was tackled by Georgia's Johnny Henderson, who weighed 170 pounds soaking wet, for no gain.

Georgia rolled from there, winning 41–27. The headline in the Jacksonville paper the next day said it all: "Fourth-and-Dumb."

The Chandler Show

After devastating losses to Georgia in 1975 and '76, Florida needed a hero when the Gators faced the Bulldogs in 1977. His name was Wes Chandler.

Chandler was an amazing player whose talents were not used to their fullest in Doug Dickey's wishbone offense. But against Georgia in '77, Dickey turned to Chandler to try to get a win. The receiver responded with the game's first score on a spectacular one-handed catch in the back of the end zone. He ran for two more scores after being shifted to tailback and led the Gators to a 22–17 win over the hated Bulldogs.

There was something about Georgia that brought out the best in wide receiver Wes Chandler, who scored this touchdown against the Bulldogs in 1976 and added three touchdowns the following year in a 22–17 win.

Jimmy Du

When Florida faced Auburn in 1973, Doug Dickey decided to make several changes in his backfield. One of them was to insert a 5'11" sophomore at fullback. Two years later, Jimmy DuBose would have a dream season.

As a sophomore and junior DuBose was more of a blocker than a legitimate threat, but he exploded during his senior year. In the Gators' wishbone offense, the basic play was for quarterback Don Gaffney to stick the ball in DuBose's middle and read the defense. Defenders, worried about the Gators' speedy halfbacks, would often overpursue, and Gaffney would let DuBose keep it.

The result was one of the best seasons ever for a Florida back. DuBose ran for 1,307 yards in 1975 and averaged 6.8 yards on his 191 rushing attempts. Affectionately known by fans as "Jimmy Du," DuBose is still third all-time at UF in yards in a season, and his 204 yards against Florida State in 1975 is the fifth best total for the Gators.

In that 1975 season, DuBose's efforts were good enough for him to be named the SEC's player of the year. He was Florida's first recipient of the award since Steve Spurrier had won it in 1966.

A typical play for DuBose that year came against Vanderbilt. Gaffney stuck the ball in his belly, then left it there after reading the defense. DuBose broke through the line, and a Commodore linebacker ran right past him thinking the play was going outside to the right. DuBose ran 80 yards for a score on the play.

In his final season, the student section began to serenade DuBose on his birthday—October 25—as the Gators were playing Duke. The Gators were lined up for a punt but faked it, snapping the ball to DuBose, who picked up the first down while the students were still singing.

Jimmy DuBose was inserted at fullback during the Auburn game in 1973, but it was in 1975 that he made his biggest impact. He rushed for more than 1,000 yards in Doug Dickey's wishbone offense.

Give 'Em Hell, Pell

Charley Pell's teams struggled against Georgia. They suffered what is considered one of the most difficult losses in UF history in 1980.

When Charley Pell took over as Florida's new coach in 1979, he found a program in disarray. The facilities were in poor shape, the boosters were disorganized, and the team was lacking in talent.

Pell went at the task of getting Florida football back on its feet with the energy of a teenager. He toured cities all around the state to organize Gator Clubs—groups of fans who would donate to the school. He created the Bull Gators, big-money boosters who would achieve that status with only the largest of donations. And he pushed for a new weight room, locker room, and stadium expansion.

On the field, it didn't go so well for Pell in his first season. He didn't win a game. Florida lost All-SEC linebacker Scot Brantley to a head injury in the second game of the season and never recovered, going 0–10–1. That team had five different starting quarterbacks during the season, leaving Pell searching for an answer.

He also had to deal with a lack of discipline on the team. When he confiscated marijuana from a player's room on the Friday night before a game, the player showed up the following Monday demanding his pot.

"That was the year I was introduced to the Drug Enforcement Agency," Pell said.

But Pell worked his magic in recruiting. He was the Great Persuader, whether it was with a booster or a recruit. In 1980, the team completed the greatest turnaround in NCAA history by going 8–4.

Pell had put together an all-star staff that included Mike Shanahan (who would later coach the Denver Broncos) and went after top recruits in the state of Florida. At one point he asked his sports information director John Humenik to create a glossy recruiting pamphlet to give to all recruits. When Humenik asked Pell which department to charge the costs to, Pell took a drag on his Vantage cigarette and said, "Sheesh, charge it to winning."

Pell's recruiting allowed him to put together some of the most dynamic talent

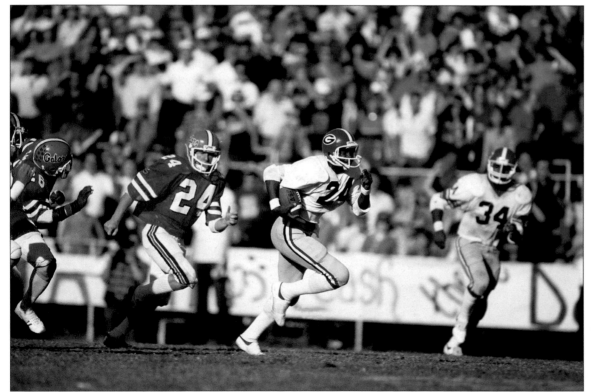

Florida had ever seen. At times, however, he coached tight in games, not wanting to take risks that could lead to turnovers. His teams had some of the greatest wins in Florida history as well as some of the most deflating defeats. Most notable was the last-second loss to Georgia in 1980 on a 93-yard pass from Buck Belue to Lindsay Scott.

He could be both charming and intimidating. He hosted socials for the media at a nearby hotel after games, but his growling voice would make a reporter tremble if something unkind was written about the Gators.

Pell helped make Florida football what it is today. He just couldn't stay around long enough to see it happen.

The Scandal

Just when Charley Pell seemed to have things under control at Florida, everything started to crumble. NCAA investigators came to Gainesville in March 1982, and newspapers jumped on the story. When it became clear the NCAA had found violations by the coaching staff, Pell wrote a letter of resignation that would take effect at the end of the 1984 season.

But when the NCAA announced 107 violations after the third game of that season, Pell was fired. The allegations included graduate assistant coaches spying on other teams, the existence of a slush fund, and players selling tickets for large amounts to eager boosters.

Pell couldn't get back into coaching in college and spent one year coaching a high school team in Florida. In 1994, he attempted suicide and was treated for mental illness. Pell eventually turned around his life, but cancer dealt a final cruel blow. He passed way in 2001 at the age of 60.

He was driven to the point of breaking the rules, and that eventually caught up with Charley Pell. After a long investigation by the NCAA, Pell resigned just three games into the 1984 season.

The Turnaround

After a 0–10–1 season, Florida fans weren't discouraged. They still flocked to Florida Field in large numbers because they believed they finally had the right man for the job. By his second season, Charley Pell had proven them right.

The 1980 Gators won eight games, including the Tangerine Bowl where they defeated Maryland 35–20. Sophomore quarterback Bob Hewko led the charge early and was replaced by true freshman Wayne Peace when Hewko suffered a season-ending knee injury against LSU.

Offensively challenged the previous year, Pell brought in Mike Shanahan to coach the offense, and it immediately paid dividends. The Gators scored 86 points in their first two games. Finally, wide receiver Cris Collinsworth had a coordinator and quarterbacks who could get him the ball. Collinsworth responded by being named All-American and the MVP of the Tangerine Bowl.

Florida also had a sure-footed kicker in Brian Clark, who kicked a game-winner as time expired to beat Kentucky 17–15. And the defense, led by linebacker David Little, kept the Gators in every game.

Although the regular season ended on a down note with a 17–13 loss at Florida State, Pell told his team in the locker room after the game that they would never lose to the Seminoles again. Under Pell, they never did.

The Class of '80

Charley Pell and his staff knew the Gator football team needed players, and in 1980 they brought in a class that would be the nucleus of the next four seasons.

Florida signed four quarterbacks that year and one of them—Wayne Peace from Lakeland, Florida—would be a starter off and on for four seasons. Another, Roger Sibbald, would become an effective defensive back. Also signed were defensive backs Tony Lilly, who would be a four-year starter at safety, and Vito McKeever.

Tailback Lorenzo Hampton ended up being a first-round pick by the Miami Dolphins, and wide receiver Dwayne Dixon led the Gators in receiving in 1982 and '83.

But the big signing was tight end Wilber Marshall. Marshall played tight end his first year, then switched to outside linebacker, where he was an All-American. He is now one of the five members of Florida's Ring of Honor.

Charley Pell's second recruiting class turned things around at Florida, thanks in part to the arrival of Wilber Marshall. Marshall came to UF as a tight end but moved to outside linebacker, where he became one of the most dominant players in college football.

Dramatic Wins in '82

One of the most interesting seasons in Florida history was 1982, when UF beat Miami on James Jones's spectacular catch and handled Southern Cal 17–9. The latter win prompted Charley Pell (pictured) to lead the team in a victory lap around Florida Field.

Charley Pell's 1982 team finished the season with an 8–4 record, but it was not without high drama. Two of the victories in that season are still two of the most talked about in Gator history.

The first came on opening day, September 4, when the Gators took on rival Miami at Florida Field. The Hurricanes had won four straight against Florida, but on a steamy day in Gainesville, a play now simply known as "The Catch" would become a part of Gator lore.

Florida trailed late 14–10 when junior quarterback Wayne Peace drove Florida to the Miami 17-yard line. He called a naked bootleg play and was looking for wide receiver Dwayne Dixon on a drag route. But at the last minute, he spotted running back James Jones downfield.

"I thought [the ball] was going to go over my head," Jones said. "I started to backpedal and just stretched for it. It hit my hand and palm perfectly."

Jones landed at the Miami goal line, and the official signaled a touchdown with 1:18 to play. Florida's defense held, and the Gators had a big win.

Trojan quarterback Sean Salisbury saw enough of Wilber Marshall (88) during the 1982 Florida–Southern Cal game. Marshall was a one-man wrecking crew, leading Florida to a 17–9 win.

But an even bigger win was coming the next week. USC had never brought a team to Gainesville and hasn't since. But on this day, Wilber Marshall became a legend. The Trojans kept running their famous student body left play, a sweep that stranded the linebacker on the other side of the field unblocked. But few linebackers could run like Marshall.

He finished the game with 14 tackles and single-handedly neutralized the USC offense in a 17–9 Florida win. After the game, Pell led the team in a victory lap around the stadium in front of delirious fans.

"I didn't go back out there," Marshall said. "I was beat."

Pell's Best

With Bernie Kosar (20) at quarterback, Miami's 1983 team would win a national championship. But the Hurricanes were no match in the opener against the Florida Gators, losing 28–3 in Gainesville.

As the 1983 season began, optimism was high in Gainesville. Florida's recruiting class of 1980 was now a group of weathered seniors looking to make their mark in the SEC and on the national landscape.

And they started with a bang. The Gators hammered Miami 28–3 in the opener. That Miami team would go on to win the national championship in '83.

The following week, Florida appeared to have recorded a second straight win over Southern Cal, then seemed to have lost it. The final verdict was neither. A Trojan incompletion on the last play of the game looked as if it would give Florida a 19–13 win. But safety Tony Lilly was flagged for a late hit on the play, and USC was given a second chance. This time, Southern Cal scored but missed the extra point, and the game ended up in a tie.

Florida rolled from there, winning its next five games. But on the plains of Auburn, the Gators suffered their first loss, 28–21. One of the key plays was a Neal Anderson fumble at the goal line. Charley Pell was so incensed at the call and several others that he blasted the officials in his postgame press conference.

The following week, Florida suffered another debilitating loss to Georgia 10–9 when the Bulldogs drove the length of the field to win it late. Another questionable—and crucial—call was when Wilber Marshall jumped over a pile and caught his foot on the helmet of a Georgia player. Marshall was called for a late hit penalty that kept the Georgia drive alive.

Florida finished the regular season with a 53–14 destruction of Florida State and then went to the Gator Bowl. On a windy, cold night in Jacksonville, the Gators finished their 9–2–1 season with a 14–6 win over Iowa. The winning score came on a high snap to the Iowa punter that linebacker Doug Drew corralled in the end zone.

Neal Anderson (27) almost quit the team as a freshman because of a lack of playing time. He went on to become one of the best Gator tailbacks in the school's history, rushing for 835 yards in 1983.

SEC Champs—At Last

With running back John L. Williams (22) leading the way, Florida beat Auburn in 1984 on its way to its first SEC championship. That title was later stripped by the league, but the players still have their rings.

After coming so close so many times, Florida won its first SEC title in 1984. But it wasn't Charley Pell who took the team he built to the title.

After the NCAA announced 107 violations against Florida three games into the season, UF pulled the plug on Pell. He was forced to resign with a 1–1–1 record and was replaced by offensive coordinator Galen Hall. Hall was the opposite of Pell, a laid-back and congenial fellow who was thrust into the spotlight. But he also coached without some of the tightness that enveloped Pell.

Florida had plenty of talent, but injuries at quarterback had forced the Gators to go with a walk-on freshman quarterback named Kerwin Bell. When Pell was ousted and Hall took over, it was like a black cloud had been lifted from the team.

"I think it pulled us together," Bell said.

Florida didn't lose again. The Gators crushed Auburn 24–3 and beat Georgia 27–0 with fans pouring onto the field in the Gator Bowl after the win. On November 17 in Lexington, Kentucky, Adrian White's interception late in the game secured a 25–17 win over Kentucky and gave Florida the SEC crown the Gators had wanted for so long.

In the radio booth, Florida sports information director and color commentator Norm Carlson said into his microphone, "Oh, Adrian. You have no idea what you just did."

Stripped of the SEC Crown

Because Florida was on probation from the NCAA, the 1984 team could not play in a bowl. On April 3, 1985, the SEC's executive committee decided to allow UF to keep its SEC title because it had been punished enough. But a month later at the conference's spring meetings, Tennessee moved to have the SEC title taken away from Florida. The presidents of the schools that make up the SEC voted 6–4 to vacate the title for 1984.

"Everyone knows who won it on the field," quarterback Kerwin Bell said. "We still have the rings."

Florida did honor the '84 team in 1997 when the school's national championship and SEC titles were painted on the wall in the south end zone. It says, "First in the SEC 1984 1985 1990." The '85 and '90 teams also were ineligible to compete for the league championship. Those years, however, were removed from the wall for space reasons when Florida won its second national title.

Gator fans can go to extremes to show their feelings for Florida football, even using a Gator coin bank to take care of spare change. An angry Albert awaits the next deposit.

This pennant for the 1983 Gator Bowl shows the old logo of Albert the Alligator that was used until 1994.

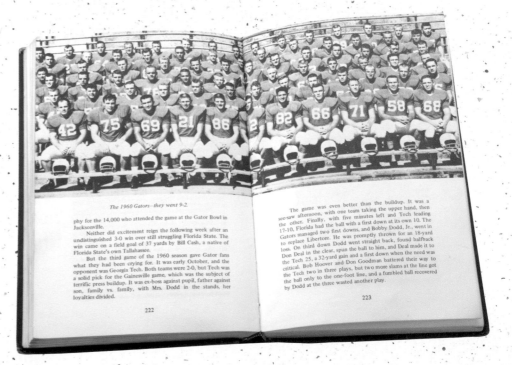

The 1960 Gators–they went 9-2.

The history of the Florida football team through the 1973 season was chronicled by longtime *Tampa Tribune* sports columnist Tom McEwen in his book *The Gators*.

It's always Gator time with a watch that displays the Florida logo. The Gator head has been synonymous with the program for the last 15 years.

Mr. Potato Head throws a mean stiff arm when he's decked out in Gator gear. The Gator script on the side of the helmet arrived at UF when Charley Pell became the Florida coach in 1979.

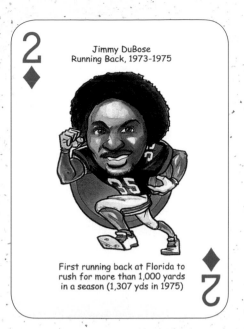

2

Jimmy DuBose
Running Back, 1973-1975

First running back at Florida to rush for more than 1,000 yards in a season (1,307 yds in 1975)

A Jimmy DuBose playing card brings back memories of the best years of the Doug Dickey era. Led by DuBose and his 1,307 rushing yards, the 1975 team was Dickey's best.

Student tickets allow UF students into games, where they occupy the southeast portion of Ben Hill Griffin Stadium and instigate the white noise heard when the opponent has the ball.

Tailgating is an art form at Florida, and a Gator ice bucket is an essential for mixing drinks. This Gator logo was changed because some people in the Florida administration joked that Albert had "chicken feet."

Laid-back Galen

When Galen Hall decided to accept Charley Pell's offer to leave Oklahoma and be the offensive coordinator at Florida, he had no idea what he was about to encounter. And really, how could Hall have predicted that just four games into his first season at UF he would be the Florida interim head coach?

After Pell's forced resignation, UF athletic director Bill Carr decided on Hall mainly because the other coaches still on staff had NCAA allegations pending. "Joe Kines was the defensive coordinator, and he had one minor allegation," Carr said. "The climate was such that you were either guilty or not charged."

Hall's demeanor combined with the talent Pell had accumulated created a perfect storm. The Gators won out after Pell's dismissal and captured their first SEC title. After the win over Kentucky, UF took the interim tag off and Hall was simply the Gators' head coach.

Carr interviewed three coaches for the job—Hall and former Gator players Lindy Infante and Steve Spurrier. Infante and Spurrier were both coaching in the United States Football League at the time.

"I told Steve he'd be the coach at Florida one day," Carr said. "But there were a third of the people who wanted Galen, a

Florida's teams in 1984 and '85 were among the best in the country, with Galen Hall loosening up the offense and taking advantage of Kerwin Bell's passing ability.

> "Galen Hall was a good man. He stepped in and did the best he could for the University of Florida."
>
> **UF athletic director Bill Carr**

third who wanted Charley Pell to come back, and a third who were split between Lindy and Steve. I told Steve he didn't want to start at Florida with only 16 percent of the people in his corner. He didn't agree and he kind of resented it. He does to this day. But I did Steve a huge favor by not hiring him."

Hall's second year at Florida was another 9–1-1 season in 1985. But by his third year, the NCAA penalties inflicted on the program began to make an impact. Because of a loss of 20 scholarships and the postseason ban, Florida wasn't as attractive to recruits as it had been before. "By 1987, we had guys starting who shouldn't have been playing," quarterback Kerwin Bell said.

Despite the presence of Emmitt Smith, the Gators struggled to a 17–12 record in Hall's last 29 games. But Hall was still a hit with the media and beloved by fans. He hosted golf outings with sportswriters around the state and had the media up to a suite in the stadium for beers and snacks after big wins. The fans gave him a long leash because of what happened in 1984 and '85. He finished his career at Florida with the best record of any Gator coach before Steve Spurrier at 40–18–1.

"Galen Hall was a good man," Carr said. "He stepped in and did the best he could for the University of Florida. He had that laid-back demeanor that enabled him to handle a stressful season. The players rallied around that lack of intensity."

Another Coach Gone

The NCAA was back in town in 1988 and '89 looking at the Florida basketball program. In the process, the organization turned up some minor violations against Galen Hall.

Hall had paid some assistant coaches bonuses out of his own pocket. The NCAA also alleged he sent money in an envelope to Palatka, Florida, for defensive back Jarvis Williams to pay child support. Hall denies facts surrounding the latter allegation to this day.

But he agreed to resign because of the allegations. He wanted to coach the rest of the season, but UF officials decided the fifth game of the season would be his last.

On October 8, less than 24 hours after a gutsy 16–13 win over LSU, Florida announced that the Galen Hall era was over. Gary Darnell would be the interim coach.

Galen Hall came to Florida from Oklahoma to be the offensive coordinator but soon was thrust into the job as interim head coach after Charley Pell was forced to leave. He led the Gators to eight straight wins in his first season but eventually also had to resign because of NCAA violations.

Alive in '85

As good as Florida's football team was in 1984, the team the following year was probably better. Quarterback Kerwin Bell had a year under his belt, the defense was rock solid, and the NCAA investigation was in the rearview mirror. The biggest problem was what that investigation left in its wake. Florida could not play in a bowl game or win the SEC title because of sanctions imposed by college sports' governing body.

Although they were ineligible for a bowl game because of NCAA sanctions, the 1985 Gators enjoyed the school's first No. 1 ranking after a tough win at Auburn 14–10.

But the Gators didn't let it affect their play on the field. They hammered Miami 35–23 to start the season. What followed was a bizarre tie against Rutgers at home. Hall felt a 28–0 lead was enough and inserted backup Rodney Brewer into the game. Brewer threw an interception for a touchdown, and Rutgers came storming back to tie the game.

The Gators recovered to win six straight, capped by a 14–10 win at Auburn that featured Ray McDonald making a circus catch in the end zone for the game-winner against Bo Jackson's Tigers. The win elevated UF to its first-ever No. 1 ranking and to the cover of *Sports Illustrated*.

Next came the annual game with Georgia in Jacksonville. The Bulldogs were stinging after a 27–0 loss the year before and were salivating over the thought of knocking the Gators out of the top spot.

And that's exactly what they did. Georgia's defense bottled up the Florida running attack and put pressure on Bell. With the Bulldogs leading 17–3 and Florida driving, Bell's pitch to running back John L. Williams hit him in the chest and fell to the ground. Georgia recovered and scored one play later. Bulldogs fans stormed the field and fighting broke out. Some even attacked Albert the Alligator. It was the last time fans were allowed onto the field following a Florida–Georgia game.

Florida finished the season 9–1–1.

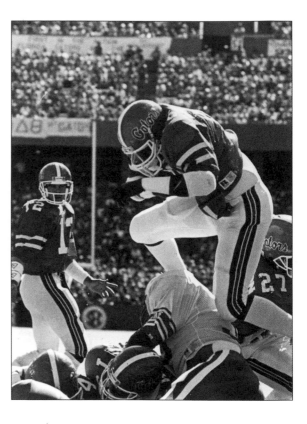

The 1985 Gator team featured a two-pronged running attack with John L. Williams and Neal Anderson gobbling up yards on the way to a 9–1–1 season.

Albert and Company

The football stadium at Florida took on a new name in 1989 thanks to a $20 million donation by citrus magnate Ben Hill Griffin. Ben Hill Griffin Stadium has had two more expansions since then, driving the capacity to 92,000.

The University of Florida's football teams had been the Gators for more than six decades, but it wasn't until 1970 that a gator mascot showed up. His name was (and is) Albert, a green, orange, and blue 7' alligator. Albert doesn't speak but rather pantomimes his thoughts during athletic events. He was joined by Alberta, the female version of the mascot, in 1986.

Florida also brought to the football stadium a different twist in the early 1980s. The 1980 movie *Alligator* featured a giant reptile that lived in the Chicago sewers. When the movie was completed, the fake alligator used in the film was given to UF. Engineering students tried to figure out a way to make the 30' long alligator walk on its own but failed. Instead, the gator was pulled around the stadium with smoke coming out of its nose.

By then, Florida Field looked nothing like it did originally. The south end zone had been filled in to make the stadium a finished bowl and increase capacity to 72,000. With the expansion came upgrades of the locker room and weight room.

One of the boosters who had been recruited heavily by Charley Pell when he arrived at Florida was citrus grower Ben Hill Griffin Jr., whom Pell referred to as Mr. Ben Hill. Griffin wrote a check to UF for more than $20 million, and in 1989 the stadium was renamed Ben Hill Griffin Stadium, although the playing surface is still called Florida Field.

Florida fans were loyal even during the Gators' most difficult season. The stadium was nearly full during the 0–10–1 season of 1979.

There were several representations of the alligator during Florida's history before the school settled on Albert as the official mascot in 1970. Albert is seen here at the 1985 Auburn game.

Run, Emmitt, Run!

College football recruiting back in the mid-1980s was hardly the cottage industry it is today, with Internet sites and newsletters leaving no player unranked. That all began to change, however, with the recruitment of Emmitt Smith.

The running back from Pensacola had fans from around the country buzzing. Where would he go? On signing day he showed up wearing Nebraska colors. But he chose Florida. So many calls came in wondering about his decision that newspapers around the state set up answering machines to deal with the influx of calls.

Smith barely played in Florida's first game and ran for one touchdown in the second. But it was in his third game that the college football world realized there was more to Smith than just hype. He ran for 224 yards on 39 carries to lead the Gators to a 23–14 win over Alabama in Birmingham.

With Smith and Kerwin Bell, the Gators should have been one of the nation's better teams in 1987. But the probation that had taken 20 scholarships away from the Gators over two years had taken its toll. Florida went 6–6, losing to Troy Aikman's UCLA team in the Hula Bowl.

Smith continued to amaze during the following season in 1988. His 96-yard touchdown run against Mississippi State is still considered one of the best ever at UF. Smith took a handoff and appeared to be stopped for a short gain. Instead, he kept his balance and came flying out of the pile, outrunning the Bulldog defenders to the end zone.

Smith was never the fastest guy on the field. But he never was caught from behind. One recruiting analyst,

Emmitt Smith took Florida football by storm as a freshman in 1987, and by his junior year Smith was a Heisman candidate. Despite a mediocre season for the team, Smith finished seventh in the 1989 voting.

Although an injury kept him from duplicating his numbers from his freshman season, Emmitt Smith still managed 988 yards as a sophomore in 1988 and averaged 5.3 yards a carry.

Max Emfinger, said Smith was a "plugger" who would never play in the NFL. Instead, he became the all-time NFL rushing leader.

Some of Smith's success can be attributed to his remarkable sense of balance, some to his keen vision. He also knew how to conserve energy, waiting until an opposing player or a teammate offered a hand to help him off the ground.

After his junior season, Smith had a decision to make. New coach Steve Spurrier was coming in, and Smith was thinking about the NFL. He wanted to hear from Spurrier that he was wanted, but Spurrier's style was never to beg players to return for their final seasons. Feeling slighted by the new coach, Smith bolted for the NFL..

Even though Florida only played in three second-tier bowl games during his three years as a Gator, Smith's legacy is monumental. He was one of four players named to the original Ring of Honor and was named to *The Gainesville Sun*'s Team of the Century in 1999.

The Records

One of Emmitt Smith's long-standing records was eclipsed in 2008 when Tim Tebow sped past Smith's mark of 36 rushing touchdowns. Tebow also broke the record for rushing touchdowns in a season, which Smith shared with Buford Long at 14. His career-rushing total of 3,928 yards was beaten in 1993 by Errict Rhett, who played four years to Smith's three.

But Smith still has plenty of records at UF, including:

• Rushing yards per game in a career: 126.7

• 100-yard rushing games: 23

• Consecutive 100-yard rushing games: 8

• Longest run from scrimmage: 96 vs. Mississippi State in 1988

• Rushing yards in a game: 316 vs. New Mexico in 1989

By the time Emmitt Smith was finished at the University of Florida, he had rushed for nearly 4,000 total yards and ran for at least 100 yards in more than 20 games. Smith left UF after his junior season and went on to become the NFL's all-time leading rusher.

Stars of the '70s and '80s

It says a lot about the 1970s and '80s that 60 percent of Florida's Ring of Honor (Jack Youngblood, Emmitt Smith, and Wilber Marshall) came from those two decades. But if the University Athletic Association's criteria for the Ring were not so restrictive, the two decades would have produced a plethora of candidates.

Carlos Alvarez ranks among the top of all-time great Gator receivers. He also made the SEC All-Academic team from 1969 through 1971.

Start with John Reaves and Carlos Alvarez, who formed one of the great pass duos in the history of the school. Reaves set the NCAA record for passing yards in a career, and Alvarez had the UF record for career receptions until it was broken in 2007 by Andre Caldwell.

Alvarez was hardly the only wide receiver to shine during this period, as both Wes Chandler and Cris Collinsworth were named All-Americans. And while this was the era of Emmitt Smith and perhaps Florida's finest offensive lineman ever in Lomas Brown, it was on defense that Florida players were most impressive during the two decades.

The list of linebackers is enough to make a quarterback shudder: Wilber Marshall, Ralph Ortega, Alonzo Johnson, Clifford Charlton, Sammy Green, David Little. They were all named All-American.

The secondary included great players such as Jarvis Williams, a cornerback who started every game he played in for four straight seasons, and former walk-on Louis Oliver,

He wasn't heavily recruited out of Monticello, Florida, but Jack Youngblood (left) turned into one of the best players to ever suit up for the Gators. He was inducted into the Ring of Honor in 2006.

a safety who was twice named All-American. David Galloway and Trace Armstrong were two of the finest defensive tackles to play at Florida.

This was a period when defense ruled, but there were plenty of offensive stars as well. One of them who had a brief career at UF was Nat Moore. Moore came to Florida after playing junior college basketball. He was such an unknown that his first name was incorrectly spelled as "Nate" in the program for his first game. But Moore had an immediate impact. His nifty moves were the reason the stands were packed for Florida's 1972 team that went 5–5–1. His 52-yard scamper off a screen pass against Auburn saw all 11 Tigers have a shot at tackling Moore. Unfortunately, Moore suffered a knee injury and wasn't much of a factor in his senior year.

This era also saw the "Great Wall of Florida." The 1984 offensive line was given that nickname because it was so effective at paving the way for running backs Neal Anderson and John L. Williams. The Great Wall was made up of center Phil Bromley, guards Brown and Billy Hinson, and tackles Crawford Ker and Jeff Zimmerman.

It was during the 1980s that Florida had two of the best kickers ever. Ray Criswell was the Florida punter from 1982 to '85 and still owns the UF career average title at 44.4 yards per

try. And Bobby Raymond, who was Florida's placekicker in 1983 and '84, remains the record holder for field goal percentage in a career at 87.8 percent.

The NFL began to discover the Gators during these two decades. Prior to 1970, Florida had three players taken in the first round of the NFL draft. From 1970 to '89, Florida had 16, including three—Armstrong, offensive tackle David Williams, and Oliver—in the first round of the 1989 draft. In all, 84 players from Florida were drafted during this era, and 10, Florida's most ever, were taken by the NFL in the 1978 draft.

As a sophomore, John Reaves (7) teamed up with Carlos Alvarez to form a dangerous passing duo. By the time Reaves was finished at UF, he had set the NCAA record for passing yards in a career.

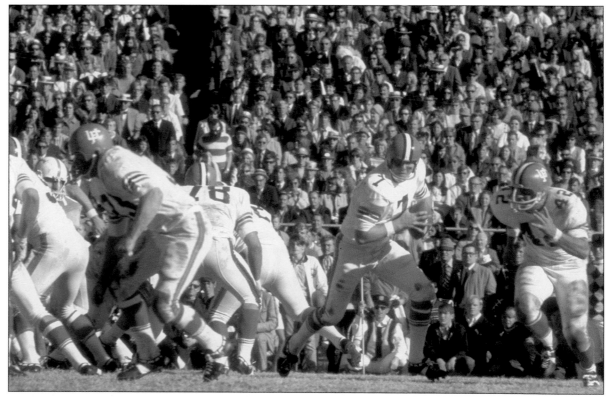

Hall's Last Dance

Galen Hall, here greeting FSU coach Bobby Bowden, was caught up in an NCAA investigation of the UF basketball program. Investigators found a handful of minor violations that cost Hall his job.

It was a Thursday when two reporters from *The Gainesville Sun* showed up at Galen Hall's house unannounced. Florida, at 3–1, would face LSU in Baton Rouge in two days, but the reporters didn't want to ask Hall about the game. They wanted to ask him if he was being fired. Hall begged off, saying he would address rumors after the game. Then he went out and coached the Gators the best he could.

It turned out to be his last game as the UF head coach. On October 7, 1989, Galen Hall left the field a winner. It was a remarkable game that appeared headed for a tie.

Emmitt Smith had scored for Florida, and a defensive effort led by tackle Brad Culpepper stopped LSU on a pair of fourth-down plays. The score was tied at 13 with 1:20 to play. Kyle Morris drove the Gators down the field, and Florida tried to surprise LSU with a draw play to Smith with only seconds left and no timeouts. Smith stretched the run to the right and failed to get out of bounds.

Morris rushed the team to the line and fired a pass out of bounds. But the clock read 0:00. Hall argued with officials, while LSU celebrated the

The battles between UF and LSU were tough ones during the 1980s, including a last-second win in 1989 for Florida, 16–13.

tie on the other sideline. The officials eventually put one second on the clock. Arden Czyzewski, in because starting kicker John David Francis had missed earlier in the game, came in and made a 41-yard field goal that barely snuck inside the left upright for the 16–13 win.

"After the game, Galen got really emotional and we had no idea what to think," Culpepper said.

The following day, it was announced that Hall had been fired and would be replaced on an interim basis by Gary Darnell, the team's defensive coordinator.

Ups and Downs

After Florida beat LSU in Baton Rouge in 1989, defensive coordinator Gary Darnell was basking in the victory. He had no idea how his life would change a day later.

Galen Hall had kept it from his staff that the LSU game would be his last, so Darnell was floored when he was told on Sunday that he was the interim head coach for UF. He found out the news when someone who had been on a previous coaching staff with Darnell called him.

Darnell had been brought in by Hall to shore up the defense in 1988; the Gators led the conference and were third in the nation that year. His 1989 defense finished third again. But the offense, which had been mostly Emmitt Smith runs, lost its only other real threat that season.

One day after Darnell recorded his first win as Florida interim head coach—a 34–11 win against Vanderbilt—Florida lost its starting quarterback. On October 15, Florida suspended quarterback Kyle Morris and three other players for betting on games.

Athletic director Bill Arnsparger had received an anonymous letter about the gambling and acted. The players would be suspended for the remainder of the year. They were reinstated by the NCAA after the season, but the damage was devastating.

Florida barely survived a homecoming game against the University of New Mexico, winning 27–21 thanks to Smith's school-record 316 rushing yards. The Gators were 6–1 and ranked 19th in the nation, but the teeth of the schedule remained.

On November 4, the Gators led Auburn 7–3 late in the game. With all that Florida and Darnell had been through, this would be a soothing victory over the 12th-ranked team in America. But with 26 seconds to play on fourth-and-ten, Auburn quarterback Reggie Slack found receiver Shayne Wasden open in the end zone for the winning score from 25 yards out. The loss was devastating to a team that had fought so hard and dealt with so much adversity. The Gators lost the next week to Georgia, beat Kentucky, and then lost to Florida State.

Florida's 1989 season ended with a thud, a 34–7 loss to Washington in the Freedom Bowl. Quarterback Donald Douglas (pictured) ran for a score on Florida's first play of the game, but that was all the Gators could manage offensively.

RESERVED PARKING

GATORS. FANS ONLY

FLORIDA GATORS
VOLS
TENNESSEE VOLUNTEERS

OCT. 13, 1984   TBA
$14.00
PRICE - TAXES INCL.
168268
21 Y7 22 6
GATE SEC. ROW/BX SEAT

Back in 1984, you could buy a ticket to see Florida and Tennessee play in Knoxville for a mere $14. It costs considerably more today, whether it's a home or away game.

This sign might not work, especially in Tallahassee or Knoxville, but it's worth a try. This is the kind of item Florida fans love to display as part of the Gator Nation.

FLORIDA
XIIth ANNUAL ALL AMERICAN BOWL vs. ILLINOIS
December 29, 1988 • Legion Field • Birmingham, AL

RB Emmitt Smith
DT Trace Armstrong
DT Rhondy Weston
OT David Williams
MG Jeff Roth
FS Louis Oliver
ALL AMERICAN BOWL

A Florida media guide from the All-American Bowl in Birmingham, Alabama, highlights great Gators such as Trace Armstrong, Louis Oliver, and Emmitt Smith.

For Florida fans, going to a game often means wearing a pin to show support for the Gator team. This old-school pin shows Albert with clenched fists, ready for action.

FLORIDA GATORS
F

Uno has been around since 1971 and is one of the most popular family card games around. It gained even more popularity in the Gator Nation when it became Gator Uno.

He's a happy gnome now that he's decked out in his Gator gear, right down to his blue sneakers. Placed in a garden, this gnome will ward off insects, birds, and Seminoles.

This postcard shows the old Albert logo along with Ben Hill Griffin Stadium before its last two renovations took capacity to more than 90,000.

Coca-Cola has had plenty of opportunities to come out with commemorative bottles honoring UF teams, such as this one for the '84 SEC champs.

GLORY DAYS

1990–2008

Until the arrival of Steve Spurrier as the coach of the Florida Gators, the football program had everything in place to be successful but nothing official to show for it. That was about to change. Drastically. The happy times were finally within reach for all Gators everywhere. SEC titles that were so elusive were about to become expected. And the first national championship was just around the corner.

Left: *His midseason promise delivered, Florida quarterback Tim Tebow waves to the predominantly Gator crowd after being named the offensive MVP of the 2008 BCS National Championship Game in Miami's Dolphin Stadium.*
Far left: *The cover of* Sports Illustrated *tells the story for the 2006 Gator football team and its quarterback Chris Leak. "We'll be connected at the hip forever," Florida coach Urban Meyer said of his quarterback. Leak was at his best in the title matchup against Ohio State, managing the game brilliantly in the 41–14 win.*

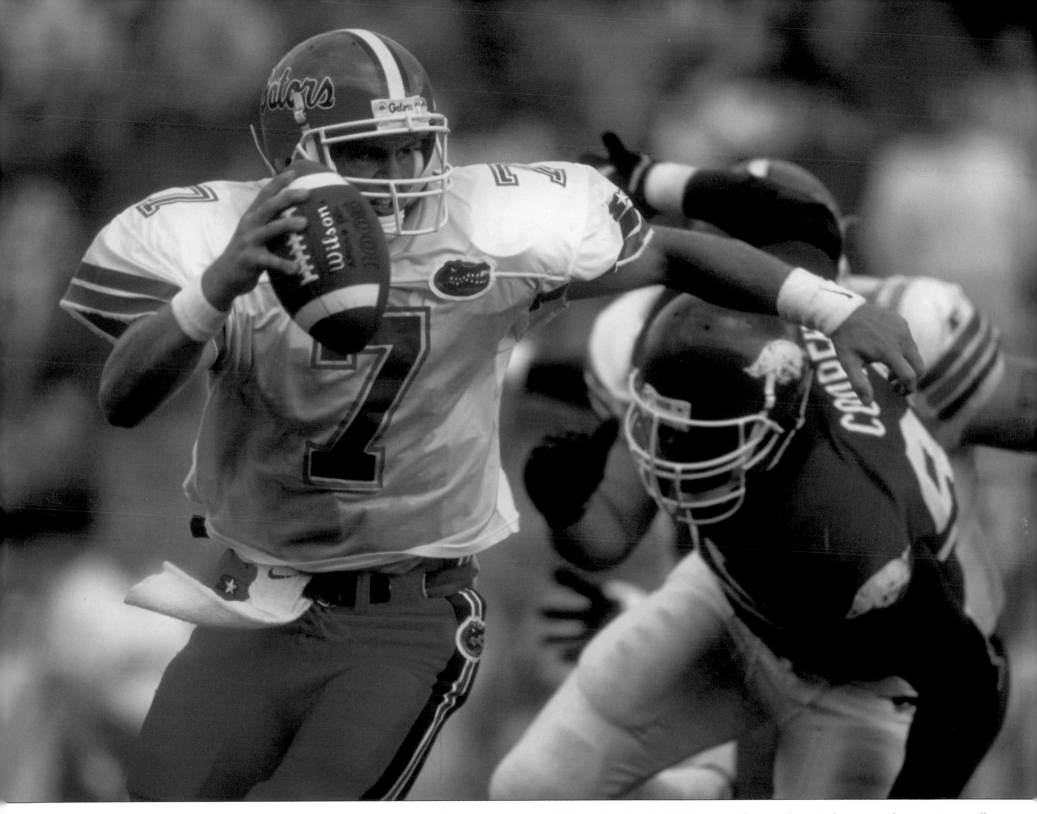

Although he was known for his precision passing, quarterback Danny Wuerffel could move around the pocket when he had to. Here, he avoids an Arkansas rusher in Fayetteville during UF's 42–7 win in 1996. During the game, Wuerffel broke the school record for career passing yards, a record broken five years later by Rex Grossman.

Spurrier to the Rescue

Steve Spurrier (center) and Danny Wuerffel (right) had a special bond. Wuerffel shared the quarterback duties with Terry Dean for two seasons before taking over the reins in 1995 and shattering all of the Gator passing records under Spurrier's tutelage.

It was New Year's Eve, 1989, when a press conference was called at the Gator Room in Ben Hill Griffin Stadium. After weeks of speculation, Steve Spurrier was introduced as Florida's coach. Right away, the media knew things were going to be different.

Spurrier had a swagger, a confidence that made him different from the Gator coaches before him. He was funny and witty. He was going to change everything.

No more orange jerseys. The Gators would return to the blue they wore when Spurrier won the Heisman Trophy. "Those orange jerseys look too much like Clemson," he said.

No more artificial turf. He wanted it replaced with grass to cut down on injuries. Spurrier wanted to start playing the University of Miami again. The series had been discontinued because of disagreements about ticket allotments in 1987.

Most importantly, there would be no more excuses. "There's no reason we have to be third best in the state of Florida," Spurrier said.

And then the following spring, Spurrier

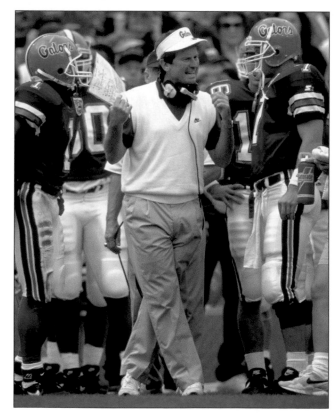

Buried on the depth chart when Spurrier arrived in 1990, Shane Matthews secured the starting job with an outstanding performance in the Orange and Blue spring game. For the next three seasons, Matthews led Florida to a 28–8 record and the school's first official SEC title.

passed along this gem when asked who his starting quarterback would be: "Whoever it is will lead the league in passing."

He wasn't kidding. Shane Matthews did just that in 1990, and the Gators had the best record in the conference. But the Gators were on probation from infractions during the Galen Hall era and were ineligible for the SEC title. Still, when Florida put the years of its SEC champions on the south end zone wall in 1997, Spurrier insisted the 1990 team go up there as well.

"That team made it possible for everything else that happened," he said.

From the first game of the season against Oklahoma State on September 8, 1990, Spurrier displayed a wide-open passing style that was foreign to the SEC. Some Florida fans were unsure that it would work in a conference that was based on running the ball and playing defense. But after a five-play drive—four of them long passes—gave Florida its first score, those fans knew they had something special.

More than anything, it was Spurrier's competitiveness that changed Florida football. In everything he did, whether it was ping-pong, golf, or coaching football, he went at it with great zeal. Spurrier was hardly a workaholic, however. There were days when he'd break up a staff meeting to take his coaches out for a quick nine holes on the golf course.

But what really made Spurrier different from anything the SEC had ever seen was his brutal honesty. He'd dig at media members, toss zingers at the opponents. When he felt quarterback Danny Wuerffel had been hit late numerous times in a loss to Florida State in 1996, Spurrier brought the members of the media who covered the Gators into a meeting room in the coaches' offices to show them the tape.

During his tenure, Florida won 122 games and six SEC titles. Everything had changed.

The Zingers

Steve Spurrier liked to get under the skin of his opponents, who took to calling him "Steve Superior" and "the Evil Genius." Some of his best quotes include:

"You can't spell Citrus without U-T" (a reference to Tennessee's frequent trips to the lower-level Citrus Bowl).

"I'm passing by the Citrus Bowl, the winter home of the Tennessee Volunteers."

"You know what FSU stands for—Free Shoes University" (this after FSU players had been exposed for getting free clothes and shoes at a store in Tallahassee).

"Statistics are for losers and assistant coaches."

After a fire gutted a library at Auburn University: "The real tragedy is that 15 of the books hadn't been colored yet."

And this after his third straight win over the University of Georgia: "How is it that every year Georgia says it had the best recruiting class but we always win the game?"

Whether it was ping-pong—where he once suffered a black eye during an intense game—golf, or coaching football, Steve Spurrier has always been one of the most intense competitors the game has ever known.

This Time, It's Official

After so many years of frustration, Florida players like defensive end Kevin Carter were able to celebrate an official SEC title in 1991 when the Gators beat Kentucky 35–26 at Florida Field.

The party spilled out onto University Avenue. Gators everywhere were hugging. Finally after coming so close so many times and having three titles stripped, there was nothing anybody could say about the 1991 SEC race.

Florida had won it.

From the 35–0 destruction of Alabama to start the SEC season to the nail-biting 35–26 win over Kentucky to close out a perfect SEC slate, Florida had clearly been the league's best team. Steve Spurrier grabbed a microphone after the game and thanked the fans—not just the ones in the stadium but also those who had supported Florida football for so long.

The fans in the stands didn't want to leave. They stayed and cheered and leaned over the wall to slap hands with players wearing T-shirts and hats that declared them champions.

"The celebration was incredible," said Shane Matthews, the quarterback who was able to do what so many quarterbacks before him could not. "It was a huge accomplishment to do it on the field, and nobody could take it away. It's something I'll always remember."

The victory also meant a trip to the Sugar Bowl, but the Gators weren't done yet. They knocked off Florida State 14–9 in a rugged defensive game. That win secured Florida's first-ever ten-win season.

The Swamp

It was after the 1991 season when coach Steve Spurrier and Norm Carlson, Florida's sports information director and longtime friend, were sitting around talking about the fact that the stadium needed a nickname. They discounted the ones that were already taken like "Death Valley" and "The Big House."

Finally, Carlson remembered that the stadium was originally built in a swampy depression.

"That's it," Spurrier said. "The Swamp." And then followed with, "Only Gators get out alive."

Although Spurrier was told by a UF athletic official that the name would never stick, it stuck like gooey swamp mud. Today, The Swamp is one of the most recognizable names in college football. And one of the toughest places to play.

First it was Florida Field, then Ben Hill Griffin Stadium. Now, it's simply known as The Swamp. The stadium where the University of Florida has been so dominant since 1990 was given its nickname by Steve Spurrier.

Taming the Dawgs

They weren't supposed to beat Georgia. Not this time. The Bulldogs had lost two in a row to Steve Spurrier, but with players such as running back Garrison Hearst and quarterback Eric Zeier, the seventh-ranked Bulldogs were expected to steamroll the struggling Gators.

Most of the players left behind by Galen Hall had graduated, and Florida had turned to true freshmen at both offensive tackle spots. That made life difficult for senior quarterback Shane Matthews.

"We were terrible," Matthews said.

The Gators had been clobbered by Tennessee 31–14 and Mississippi State 30–6 in a rare Thursday night game on October 1, 1992. They had recovered to win three in a row before heading to Jacksonville for the Florida–Georgia game.

"We weren't expected to win," Matthews said. "We just made the plays in that game. That was probably the most fun Georgia game I ever played in."

The Gators prevailed 26–24 with Matthews clinching with a big pass to Harrison Houston and then running himself on a quarterback draw for a first down when Geor-gia needed the ball for one last drive. When it was over, Florida had held Hearst, a Heisman Trophy candidate, to 41 yards on 14 carries.

This was the first year the SEC went to two divisions and 12 teams. Florida managed to beat South Carolina and Vanderbilt and went to the first SEC Championship Game in Birmingham, where it lost to Alabama 28–21.

Just to have made it to the big game and to have beaten Georgia was a confidence builder for the program. So was the fact that Florida had signed the best recruiting class in the country earlier in the year.

The best was yet to come.

One of the Gators' great tailbacks, Errict Rhett (33) is the all-time rushing leader at Florida. He carried the team in 1992 and proved to be a solid receiver as well as a strong runner.

The Amazing Run

His offense was struggling against a mighty Alabama defense in the 1994 SEC Championship Game in Atlanta's Georgia Dome, so Steve Spurrier turned to trick plays that helped Florida drive to the winning touchdown in the 24–23 win.

It started with a bang. Florida's blitz through the SEC from 1993 to '96 began on a Saturday night in Lexington, Kentucky. There was nothing about this game that would have lead anyone to believe the Gators were about to go on a 34–2 SEC run and win the next four conference championships.

Until the end.

Quarterbacks Terry Dean and Danny Wuerffel had thrown seven interceptions in the game when Florida got the ball back for one last shot. Wuerffel drove the team down the field to the 8-yard line and called "Steamers Y-7." With eight seconds left, he found walk-on wide receiver Chris Doering, a Gainesville native, alone in the end zone. Somehow, Florida had pulled off a 24–20 win, and radio

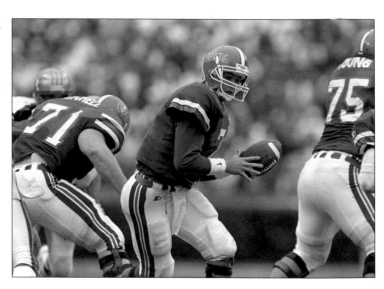

announcer Mick Hubert was screaming into his microphone: "Doering's got a touchdown! Doering's got a touchdown!"

"I remember after the game thinking of all the times the Gators had lost a game late and let me down," Doering said. "I had saved a lot of people from being let down."

Florida rolled through the rest of the season, losing only at Auburn 38–35. They beat Georgia 33–26 on a rainy day in Jacksonville when Judd Davis kicked four field goals. In the SEC Championship Game in Birmingham, Florida took care of Alabama 28–13, then hammered West Virginia in the Sugar Bowl 41–7.

The 1994 season was more of the same. Again, a loss to Auburn was the only blemish. This time, Florida needed a late drive to beat Alabama 24–23 in the first title game played in Atlanta. Steve Spurrier used some trickery on the winning drive, with Wuerffel faking an injury and then having back-up Eric Kresser throw a 25-yard pass to move the team into Tide territory. A double pass from Wuerffel to Doering to Aubrey Hill set up Wuerffel's game-winning pass to Doering from two yards out.

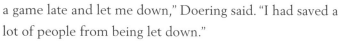

After the "Choke at Doak" in 1994, Florida needed to beat Florida State in the 1995 game to finish the regular season unbeaten for the first time in school history. Behind Danny Wuerffel's brilliance, the Gators prevailed over the sixth-ranked Seminoles 35–24.

Then came domination.

"We rolled right through them in 1995 and '96," Spurrier said. "Even the championship games weren't close."

The Gators got back at Auburn on October 14, 1995, winning 49–38 in the rain. Two turnovers allowed the Tigers to take a 10–0 lead before Reidel Anthony returned a kickoff 90 yards for a touchdown, and Florida never looked back.

The Gators destroyed the Bulldogs 52–17 on October 28, 1995, in the Florida–Georgia game, which was played in Athens, Georgia, because of construction at the Gator Bowl. By the end of the third quarter, Sanford Stadium was almost empty except for a contingent of Florida fans celebrating the win. Spurrier said after the game that he had noticed in the media guide that nobody had ever put "half-a-hundred" on Georgia in the stadium, so he went for a late score, rubbing it in to the Bulldog faithful.

Florida won the SEC title game 34–3, the highlight being a 95-yard fumble return by linebacker Ben Hanks.

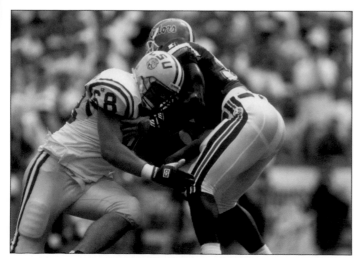

To say Steve Spurrier owned LSU during his 12 years at Florida would be an understatement. His record against the Tigers was 11–1, with the only loss coming in 1997. In this 1994 game, Florida rolled to a 42–18 win in Gainesville.

The 1996 season was Florida at its best in the SEC. The Gators jumped out to a 35–0 lead at Tennessee by the middle of the fourth quarter and hung on to win the game 35–29. Then they steamrolled Kentucky, Arkansas, Louisiana State, Auburn, and Georgia by a combined score of 261–37.

In the championship game, Florida defeated Alabama 45–30, as Anthony set the SEC record for touchdown catches in a championship game with three. But the play everybody remembers was Wuerffel's 85-yard touchdown pass to Jacquez Green after Alabama had pulled to within 31–28.

Four seasons, four rings. The SEC hadn't seen anything like it since the days of Bear Bryant at Alabama.

When Emmitt Smith left Florida a year early to enter the NFL Draft, it opened a door for running back Errict Rhett. He responded by becoming Florida's all-time leading rusher with 4,163 yards from 1990 to '93 and was a dependable receiver as well.

Fiesta Siesta

As national championship games go, it was hardly a classic. Unless you were a University of Nebraska fan, that is.

Looking back, it's hard to believe Florida actually led the 1996 Fiesta Bowl after the first quarter. The Gators were up 10–6 when the Big Red deluge hit. Nebraska scored 29 unanswered points in the second quarter and went on to rout Florida 62–24. The signature play of the game was a 75-yard touchdown run by Cornhuskers quarterback Tommie Frazier when he broke a half dozen tackles.

> "We thought we'd have a storybook ending.... But that Nebraska team was one of the greatest college teams ever."
>
> **Chris Doering**

"Going into that game, we had watched a lot of tape of Washington State's game against Nebraska," said receiver Chris Doering, who had 123 receiving yards in the game. "We felt pretty confident. But at the start of the second quarter, they exposed our blocking schemes. That was the dawn of the zone blitz in college football. We had never seen that before. It just snowballed."

Quarterback Danny Wuerffel was sacked for a safety. He threw an interception that was returned for a touchdown. By halftime, it was as good as over. The last touchdown of the game was a 93-yard kickoff return by Gator receiver Reidel Anthony, who pulled an imaginary shotgun out as he celebrated.

"We went for two and they called a slant to our outside receiver who was Travis McGriff," Doering said. "I told him I was going to take it. But I got jammed to the ground. So that was my last play in college football.

"We thought we'd have a storybook ending. I remember me and [offensive tackle] Jason Odom and Danny were the last ones in the shower. Everyone had a look of disbelief. But that Nebraska team was one of the greatest college teams ever."

Nebraska coach Tom Osborne reinstated suspended running back Lawrence Phillips (1) for the 1996 Fiesta Bowl. Phillips ran for 165 yards and scored three touchdowns in the 62–24 win.

Wuerffel Wins the Heisman

It was a close vote in 1996, but Danny Wuerffel gave Florida its second Heisman winner. His six touchdown passes in the SEC Championship Game win over Alabama swayed enough voters to get Wuerffel a place in history.

A product of the system. That's what his detractors called Danny Wuerffel. Plug a quarterback into the Steve Spurrier system and he'll put up big numbers. Forget the toughness he displayed. Forget the pinpoint passes. That's the only way the Heisman voting could be close in 1996—if enough of the more than 900 voters bought into the anti-hype.

And it was close. Even after Wuerffel, the son of a minister, had thrown 39 touchdown passes in his senior season. Even after Wuerffel had passed for 3,625 yards in 1996. Even after he threw six touchdowns to win the SEC Championship Game.

"It was pretty close," Wuerffel said. "But I think—good or bad—I just let a lot of things roll off of me. So I wasn't nervous. The whole thing was surreal almost in an overwhelming way. I went to an awards ceremony in Orlando, then another in St. Louis and then to New York."

Finally, on a cold night at the Downtown Athletic Club, the Gator Nation felt all warm and fuzzy when the announcement was made. Wuerffel edged out Iowa State running back Troy Davis, who finished second,

and Arizona State quarterback Jake Plummer, who was third. Wuerffel received 300 first-place votes, meaning he was tops on the ballots of less than a third of the voters. The margin between Wuerffel and Davis, who received 209 first-place votes, was a mere 189 points, tight by Heisman standards. (Ohio State's Troy Smith ten years later won by 1,662 points.)

The win was historic because for the first time a Heisman winner had been coached by another Heisman recipient: Steve Spurrier, who had won 30 years earlier.

Not only did Florida State win the 1996 game against Florida, but the Seminoles pounded Wuerffel. Steve Spurrier was so upset after watching the tape of the game that he called out the Seminoles for late hits on his quarterback.

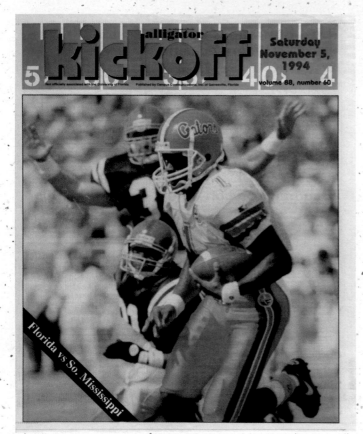

The Alligator, Florida's independent student newspaper, produces special sections for every Gator home game, including this 1994 homecoming game against Southern Miss. Florida rolled to a 55–17 win over the Golden Eagles.

After coming close in 1995 with a loss in the Fiesta Bowl, the Gators were dedicated to winning it all the following season.

You can find the Gator logo on almost anything. This poker chip is appropriate because UF's most successful coaches—Steve Spurrier and Urban Meyer—are never afraid to gamble.

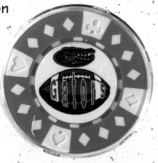

UF's 1999 media guide highlighted the tremendous decade that Steve Spurrier brought to Florida football, which included five SEC titles.

Southern Miss at Florida, 1 p.m.

The Gainesville Sun offers a special section for each Florida game, a tradition that began once the Gators started to have success in the 1990s.

This Sugar Bowl pin not only highlights the game against Notre Dame but also celebrates Florida's first-ever SEC championship.

TUESDAY, JANUARY 9, 2007   www.gainesville.com

The Gainesville Sun

FINAL AND CAMPUS EDITION   Gainesville, Florida, Vol.131, No. 182, six sections   50¢

FLORIDA 41   OHIO STATE 14

BELIEVE IT!
GATORS STUN BUCKEYES TO MAKE HISTORY

By PAT DOOLEY

ROAD TO REBIRTH, 2A | REVELRY IN THE STREETS, 2A | CHAMPIONS DESPITE ODDS, 1C | COMPLETE GAME COVERAGE, IN SPORTS

YOUR COMPLETE GAINESVILLE SUN INSIDE ◆ FOR CONTINUING GATOR COVERAGE SEE GAINESVILLE.COM AND GATORSPORTS.COM

When Florida won the 2006 national title, The Gainesville Sun produced three editions with the editors working through the night. This was the main front page delivered to readers the morning after the game.

It's not enough to own a bottle opener for tailgating. Gator fans need one that has the UF logo and plays the fight song when the top is popped.

This gold coin commemorates the 1994 season, in which Florida started the year ranked No. 1 in the nation.

The Super Season

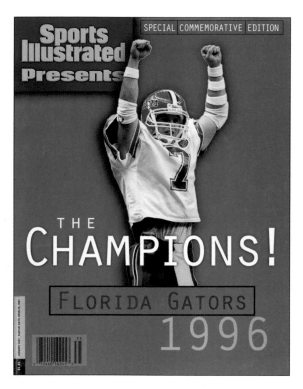

The 1997 Sugar Bowl turned out to be a national title game when Ohio State beat Arizona State in the Rose Bowl. With Danny Wuerffel throwing three touchdown passes and running for another, Florida handled Florida State 52–20 in the rematch.

The season wasn't perfect. There was a loss, a painful one both physically and mentally. But the ending? It couldn't have been any more perfect.

After so many years of trying, of firing coaches and hiring coaches, of recruiting and scandals, of stadium expansions and everything else that went into Florida football for 90 seasons, the perfect storm finally rolled in. How the Gators made it to the Sugar Bowl is almost a bigger part of the story than the actual game that brought Florida its first national championship.

It began on a rainy day in Knoxville on September 21, 1996. No. 2 vs. No. 4. Peyton Manning vs. Danny Wuerffel. The hype pelting the players on both teams all week. Then, it was the rain.

And then it happened. Steve Spurrier, always the maverick, went for it on fourth-and-13 on Florida's first possession. The result was a touchdown pass from Wuerffel to Reidel Anthony. That was the beginning of a 35–0 run just 20 minutes into the game. Tennessee rallied, but by the time they cut the score to 35–29, there was time only for a failed onside kick attempt. Most of the Volunteer faithful had already left Neyland Stadium.

"I don't know where all the Tennessee fans went," said UF linebacker James Bates, a native of Tennessee. "Maybe the *Jeff Foxworthy Show* was on."

From Knoxville, the Gators went on an amazing roll. The next five foes—Kentucky, Arkansas, LSU, Auburn, and Georgia—were outscored by a combined 261–37. Florida beat Georgia 47–7 despite the suspension of star receiver Ike Hilliard and the loss of All-SEC center Jeff Mitchell to a broken ankle on the first drive.

The 1996 Gators enter Florida Field to take on the LSU Tigers on October 12. LSU was just one of many SEC teams that were dominated by UF's amazing run that season.

Coach Spurrier celebrates on the sideline as the Gators take their first ever national championship—a 52–20 win over hated rival Florida State.

"Everything seemed to work," Wuerffel said. "We always had the right play on."

Then came Vanderbilt. During the week, Spurrier said that Vandy fans had "better not boo if our backup quarterback comes into the game and starts throwing the ball. If they do, we'll start chucking it into the end zone."

Instead, the Gators were in for a fight. Fired-up Vanderbilt trailed 28–21 late in the game, and the Gator offense was going nowhere. Not wanting to give the ball up with less than two minutes to play, Spurrier went for it on fourth-and-one. Wuerffel snuck behind guard Donnie Young and made it, just barely. Florida had survived.

The No. 1 Gators would end the regular season at Tallahassee against No. 2 Florida State on November 30. The newspaper there ran a large headline that said simply: "WAR." FSU was known for its defense, and that defense made life miserable for Wuerffel. The Seminoles prevailed 24–21. It looked like the dream of a national title were smashed.

Florida rebounded a week later to beat Alabama in the Georgia Dome 45–30 for the SEC championship. Earlier that day, the University of Texas had upset Nebraska to give the Gators hope and send them into a Sugar Bowl rematch against FSU.

The night before the game, the Gator band was marching down Bourbon Street, playing the fight song, and Gator fans were celebrating. The reason? Ohio State had taken down unbeaten Arizona State in the Rose Bowl. Florida–FSU, Part II, would be for the national title.

This time, with two healthy tackles and the shotgun formation installed to allow Wuerffel to throw the ball quicker, the Gators rolled. Florida won 52–20. The Gators celebrated deep into the night.

Trips to the White House have become common for Florida's football team (as well as the basketball teams in 2006 and 2007). Here, coach Steve Spurrier and quarterback Danny Wuerffel present President Bill Clinton with a No. 1 Florida jersey on March 27, 1997.

The Feud with FSU

It was the last game Ron Zook would coach at Florida, but he went out with a bang, beating the Seminoles 20–13. Florida had not defeated FSU at Doak Campbell Stadium since 1986. The 2004 matchup included a dedication to FSU coach Bobby Bowden.

Florida has no shortage of rivals. Tennessee, Georgia, and Miami, to name a few. But there is only one Florida State.

It was always a bitter feud. Florida was basically forced to play FSU. The Gators didn't need to. But in the 1950s, FSU coach Tom Nugent began to push the issue. When a bill in the Florida legislature that would have made the two schools play barely failed, Florida athletic director and coach Bob Woodruff knew he needed to go ahead and schedule the Seminoles.

It was a pretty sweet deal for UF. Games would be played in Gainesville with SEC officials. It wasn't until 1964 that Tallahassee hosted the game. And through the years, the heat only intensified.

Then came Steve Spurrier. The Florida coach from 1990 to 2001 was a big believer in Sun Tzu's *The Art of War.* One of the tenets from the book is: "If your opponent is temperamental, seek to irritate him." So he did.

When FSU had a scandal after its 1993 national title involving players getting free sporting goods, Spurrier started calling FSU "Free Shoes University." FSU fans called their team the 'Noles for short. Spurrier didn't buy it. He referred to them as "The Semis."

On the field, the games usually had national title implications. FSU won it all twice in the 1990s and Florida once. But one of the best games in that decade came after FSU's hopes had been dashed by Miami the week before, and Florida, while not in the mix for a national title, had won its first SEC crown. The year was 1991, and the Gators won 14–9 in Gainesville.

The game was a physical affair, with both defenses dominating. Florida led 14–3 late in the game when FSU scored. The Seminoles roared back down the field late, but a pair of passes into the end zone were tipped away at the last second.

Two years later, FSU came to Gainesville needing a win to play for a national title. Florida trailed 27–7 before coming

The matchup between Florida and FSU was intense before Steve Spurrier's arrival at UF, but when he got there the hostilities escalated. In so many families around the state, the houses were split between Gators and Seminoles.

For three quarters, Florida State had no answer for Florida in 1994. But the Seminoles rallied from a 31–3 deficit to tie the score in the end. The game is now referred to by both sides as "The Choke at Doak."

back to cut the lead to 27–21. On a third-down play with The Swamp in full throat, FSU Heisman Trophy winner Charlie Ward hit Warrick Dunn with a short pass that Dunn turned into a 79-yard touchdown to clinch the game for the Seminoles.

In 1994, the Gators looked like they would get revenge. They led 31–3 entering the fourth quarter at Doak Campbell Stadium before FSU mounted an incredible comeback, tying the game at 31. It ended that way and has been referred to ever since as "The Choke at Doak."

But arguably the best game ever played between the two teams came in 1997. Florida had lost twice in SEC play while FSU was No. 1 on the *USA Today*/ESPN poll. Spurrier decided to rotate quarterbacks Doug Johnson and Noah Brindise on every play. And it worked.

"We had nothing to lose so we were a dangerous team," Johnson said.

The game went back and forth. With only a couple minutes remaining, FSU kicker Sebastian Janikowski made a

field goal to make the score 29–25 for the 'Noles. To add insult to injury, he then did the "Gator Chomp" at Florida fans.

Florida got the ball at its own 20. Spurrier drew up a play on the sidelines, but the players weren't sure what he had called. Johnson decided to run a hitch-and-go to Jacquez Green, and it worked beautifully. One play later, Fred Taylor ran it to the 1-yard line, then punched it in on the next play. Dwayne Thomas intercepted Thad Busby on the next series to secure the game and a 32–29 Florida win.

Florida receiver Jacquez Green made what might be the signature play of the Florida–FSU series when he caught a bomb from Doug Johnson to set up the winning touchdown in Florida's incredible 32–29 victory in 1997.

Not Quite There

Florida coach Steve Spurrier made it a tradition to gather his team on the field for a photo after it won an SEC championship. Here, the Gators pose for a picture after beating Auburn 28–6 in 2000. It was Spurrier's sixth and final SEC crown at Florida.

How do you find the magic again? After Florida won the 1996 national championship, that's what fans wanted to know. The '96 team was loaded with seniors, but solid recruiting still left Florida in position to contend for national titles throughout Steve Spurrier's coaching tenure. They just were unable to get back to playing championship football.

There was one SEC crown in 2000 and an SEC Championship Game loss in 1999. But no national title games.

"We didn't have a quarterback like Danny Wuerffel," Spurrier said.

There were close calls. In 1998, Florida lost in overtime to Tennessee, and the Volunteers went on to win the national title. The 2000 team lost only to Mississippi State and FSU, both on the road.

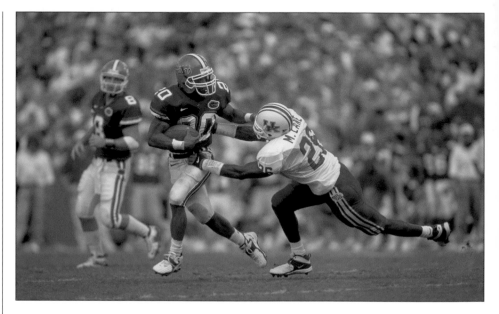

But the best team not to win it all was easily the 2001 Gators. With Rex Grossman at quarterback, it appeared Spurrier had found his man. Grossman set a Florida passing record against LSU in Baton Rouge, throwing for 464 yards in a 44–15 win. They avenged the loss to Mississippi State by winning 52–0. The scoreboard after the game blared the message, "Who shut the Dogs out?"

Florida was ranked No. 1, but with running back Earnest Graham out with an ankle injury, Florida lost at Auburn 23–20. Because of the events of 9/11, the Tennessee game had been moved to the end of the season. In Gainesville, the second-ranked Gators needed a win to play for the SEC title and a trip to the Rose Bowl for the national title game. Instead, the Vols prevailed 34–32.

"That was a great team," Spurrier said. "We had a really good defense too. They just had one bad night."

Robert Gillespie (20) was a solid running back for Florida and helped the Gators beat Kentucky 59–31 in 2000. Spurrier never lost to Kentucky during his 12 years at UF, but this game angered the head coach because of sloppy tackling. He invited the media to watch tackling drills the following Tuesday.

The Zooker

Ron Zook is carried off the field after Florida defeated Florida State 20–13 in Tallahassee in 2004. Zook was fired midseason after a loss to Mississippi State but remained as coach. He won his final three games before being hired by Illinois.

On the night before Florida was to play LSU in Baton Rouge in 2001, Florida athletic director Jeremy Foley told a small group of reporters that if Steve Spurrier, who had been flirting with NFL teams during his coaching tenure, ever left he would talk to three coaches about replacing him—former UF assistant Bobby Stoops of Oklahoma, former Gator assistant Mike Shanahan of the NFL's Denver Broncos, and former assistant Ron Zook.

The first two made sense. But Zook had been maligned as a defensive coordinator at UF and was eventually demoted by Spurrier before the 1994 season.

When Spurrier made his stunning announcement two days after the 2002 Orange Bowl that he would be leaving to pursue an NFL job, Foley went into action. He tried Stoops and Shanahan, but neither wanted to try to take the place of the most successful coach in Gator history.

So Foley went to New Orleans, where Zook was an assistant with the Saints. Zook only wanted to know one thing: "How fast can I get a cell phone to start recruiting?" he asked Foley.

The decision divided the Gator Nation. Some were happy to see Zook return. They knew he could re-cruit. Others were angry because they didn't think much of Zook when he was at Florida. Still others were simply baffled by the move.

But Zook hit the ground running. He had three straight excellent recruiting classes. When Florida won the national title in 2006, 21 of the 22 starters were Zook recruits.

On the field, the results were mixed. Zook lost games he was supposed to win. He won games he was supposed to lose. He did something Florida couldn't do with Spurrier as the coach. He won in Tallahassee. But he lost twice to Ole Miss.

He finished with a 23–14 record. Florida fans had been spoiled by Spurrier.

He Got Zooked

Two days after a devastating loss to last-place Mississippi State in 2004, Ron Zook was in the Florida weight room when he was stopped by UF athletic director Jeremy Foley and told to go to the university president's on-campus home.

"Am I in trouble?" Zook asked. He was. Florida president Bernie Machen told Zook he was fired. He would coach the rest of the season, four more games.

"Ron is a quality guy who has worked as hard as he could," Machen said at the news conference. "But it wasn't working."

It wasn't just the fact that Zook had lost in two-plus years half as many games as Steve Spurrier lost in a dozen. There was an incident between a fraternity and football players when Zook was asked to be a peacemaker by Foley. Instead, Zook got into verbal sparring with the frat boys.

"I take pride in the fact that we leave this program in very good shape," Zook said.

He was intense and passionate, and his players loved him. But Ron Zook lasted only three seasons at Florida, in part due to this controversial 30–28 loss to Tennessee in Knoxville. SEC officials later admitted to two major errors in the closing minutes of the game.

Out of Nowhere in '03

Channing Crowder watched from the sidelines, unable to play because of arthroscopic surgery the week before. He watched and grimaced as Eli Manning led Mississippi to a win over Florida. "I wanted to rip my stitches out and get out there on the field," said the Gator middle linebacker.

That loss left Florida at 3–3 in Ron Zook's second year, 2003, and the natives

Reserve linebacker Zephrin Augustine celebrates with fans after Florida's stunning 19–7 win over LSU in Baton Rouge in 2003. The Tigers would go on to win the national championship that season but couldn't handle Florida on this day.

were grumbling. Up next: sixth-ranked LSU in Tiger Stadium. No chance, right?

There was a chance after all. Crowder returned to action, and Florida's defense stifled LSU. The Gators won the game 19–7. That LSU team would go on and win the national title in 2003.

Crowder was all over the field, making tackles and getting into passing lanes to force incompletions. Florida defensive back Keiwan Ratliff picked off Matt Mauck twice, once in the fourth quarter. The Gators held LSU's running game, led by Joseph Addai, to 56 yards on 24 carries.

"You want to know how we did it?" asked UF defensive coordinator Charlie Strong. "I had Channing Crowder back on defense. He makes that much of a difference."

The game started poorly for UF when Skyler Green of LSU returned the first punt of the game 80 yards for a score. But that would be it for the Tigers. Florida's offensive coaches knew LSU liked to blitz, and the Tigers did get to freshman quarterback Chris Leak six times. But twice Leak hit tailbacks who ran past blitzers. Ran Carthon and Ciatrick Fason each caught scoring passes on the outside blitzes.

The win seemed to be a turning point for the Gators under Zook. They won their next four games before suffering a tough loss against FSU in the finale. Alas, the following season would be Zook's last.

Bobby McCray tackles LSU quarterback Matt Mauck during Florida's 19–7 win over LSU in 2003. The Tigers scored early on a punt return by Skyler Green but could muster little offense the rest of the day against the Florida defense.

All-Americans Everywhere

Jevon Kearse (42) was one of the best defensive players in Florida history. He came to UF as a safety, but the player, who teammates called "The Freak," flourished in defensive coordinator Bobby Stoops's system. In this game in 1996 against Kentucky, the Gators won 65–0.

The misconception is that it was all about offense during the Steve Spurrier era at Florida. The truth is you can't win championships without defense. And while Spurrier's teams were lighting up scoreboards around the Southeast, the Gator defenses were playing some pretty good football as well.

The best of them all was the 1998 defense. It was the last year of Bobby Stoops as the defensive coordinator. He would leave the following year to be the head coach at Oklahoma.

"That was the best defense we had there," said Spurrier. "Just couldn't find enough offense to go with it."

The leaders of that defense—linebackers Mike Peterson and Jevon Kearse—were both named to All-America teams. Kearse was nicknamed "The Freak" by teammates

because of his size, speed, and wingspan. He was a 6'4", 260-pound linebacker who would also play at defensive end with the sole purpose of batting down passes.

Among the other All-Americans on defense brought to UF by Spurrier were all-time UF interceptions leader Fred Weary, all-time sacks leader Alex Brown, future All-Pro defensive end Kevin Carter, and versatile defensive back Lito Sheppard, who also returned punts and played offense.

It was on offense, however, that the Gators piled up the All-Americans. Among them were Florida's version of The Triplets: Wide receivers Reidel Anthony, Ike Hilliard, and Jacquez Green helped Florida reach two national championship games. Each of them had a combination of blazing speed, good hands, and the ability to get open. Green, a former quarterback, was the fastest despite suffering a dislocated hip as a freshman. The other two became such a part of Gator lore that UF fans don't even use their last names. It's just "Ike" and "Reidel."

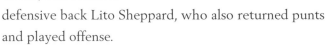

Steve Spurrier dipped into Louisiana to recruit wide receiver Ike Hilliard to Florida, and it paid off mightily. Hilliard was a force during his three seasons at Florida and teamed with quarterback Danny Wuerffel to form a lethal duo.

Party Perfection

When Urban Meyer became the Florida coach in late 2004, one of his goals was to take back Florida's home field. In this 2007 game against Tennessee, The Swamp was in full force as the Gators rolled to a 59–20 victory

The term "tailgating" comes from the days when sports fans would pull down the tailgate of a truck and plop food on it to eat before a game. At Florida, it has become an art form.

Scattered around campus, most of the 90,000 fans who attend a game have a plan. Tents are set up, tables laid out. Some of the tailgate parties come with live music. Many of them include TVs with satellite dishes.

Tailgating at Florida isn't something that starts a few hours before the game. It starts when these fans say it

starts. For night games, tents start to pop up at 8 A.M., and the grills start to fill the air with the smell of charcoal.

Every game is an event, as much a social outing as a game. Big-money boosters have their parties catered. At J. J. Finley Elementary six blocks from campus, a large field usually used for kickball and tag is converted into a giant parking lot with plenty of room for tables, chairs, food, and adult beverages. Even the area reserved for press parking becomes a big party.

Some fans prefer to enjoy restaurants along University Avenue. The Purple Porpoise was a mainstay during the 1990s and still is today under the new name "Gator City." The Salty Dog Saloon is packed hours before games. Then, there is the "other" Swamp. The Swamp Restaurant is the favorite of as many Florida fans as can be packed into the two-story building and patio area.

Fraternities on University Avenue blare music into the atmosphere. Fans can be seen carrying rolling coolers (or the latest—motorized coolers) from party to party. Private

yards within a mile of the stadium are often converted into parking spaces for as much as $35 a vehicle.

For many fans, a must-see is the Gator Walk. It is a tradition started by current coach Urban Meyer before the first game of his first season in 2005.

"I remember thinking, we're playing in one of the greatest stadiums in the country, in front of some of the greatest fans, and we're coming into our place of business and sliding into the backdoor unnoticed," Meyer said. "I thought, that's not the way we ought to do business around here. . . . If we want this to be the place that everyone truly wants to be, you don't go pulling a bus around the back of the stadium and get off the bus in sweats. You park the buses and you take the stadium the right way."

So began the Walk. Fans line up and get a chance to see their favorite players, even getting the occasional hug or

Florida's home stadium has been reinvented several times, and the high-rising bowl creates a noise machine with the help of the Gator Nation. Opponents struggle to hear signals even in the huddle because of the noise generated by UF fans.

high-five as the team exits buses and walks to the north end zone section of the stadium. With the Florida band playing the fight song, the players make their way into the stadium, descending to the field and then walking across it to their locker room in the south end zone.

The north end zone was expanded in 1991 with the addition of the Touchdown Terrace, which includes luxury boxes and club seating. At a cost of $17 million, the stadium's capacity was increased to 83,000.

Prior to the 2003 season, another expansion—this time on the west side—meant more luxury boxes and club seating to take the capacity to 90,000. And before the 2008 season, work was completed to give the stadium a new front door called the Gateway of Champions. It includes a museum dedicated to great Gator players and teams.

Part of the tradition of Gator Game Day is the Florida cheerleaders, performing here during a 2007 game against Troy. The cheerleaders induce ear-splitting cheers during games and get the Gator Chomp going.

Meyer Hire

On the day he let Ron Zook know the 2004 season would be his last as the Gators' head coach, Florida athletic director Jeremy Foley went to work. Foley and his staff started researching possible candidates to replace Zook. Thick folders full of information on different coaches were compiled. Foley wanted to know two things—interest and availability.

One of those coaches was out of a job. His name was Steve Spurrier.

Spurrier had left the Washington Redskins after two seasons and had taken a year off. He said he wanted to talk to UF about the possibility of returning. Foley and Florida president Bernie Machen tried to set up a meeting with Spurrier, but eventually he withdrew his name from consideration.

"I think it's just better they go find another coach who will be there 10 to 15 years," Spurrier said. "We had a marvelous run there for 12 years."

With Spurrier out of the picture, Foley's attention turned to Urban Meyer.

Urban Meyer runs onto the field with his Florida team for UF's 2005 game at Commonwealth Stadium in Lexington, Kentucky. This was Meyer's first road game with Florida, and his Gators jumped out to a 49–7 lead before winning 49–28.

Meyer was a hot item, a successful coach in a pair of two-year stints at Bowling Green State and the University of Utah. His Utah team was about to play in the Fiesta Bowl.

Foley flew to Utah on Thanksgiving weekend to meet Meyer. But another school had come into play for the coach—Notre Dame. The Irish had fired Tyrone Willingham, and Meyer had said previously that coaching there was his "dream job."

During a second meeting with Meyer, Foley had to leave the meeting to allow Notre Dame officials time to deliver their pitch. Foley went to a movie, shifting nervously in his seat.

"I can't tell you the plot of the movie because all I could think about [was] what was going on back at Urban's home," Foley said.

Foley returned to the Meyer home for more meetings. He also used Florida basketball coach Billy Donovan and Donovan's wife, Christine, to help recruit the Meyers.

Finally, at the Meyer dinner table, the coach-to-be said, "I'm

Fans spell out Urban Meyer's last name during a 2007 game against Florida Atlantic. With two national titles already to his credit, Meyer quickly became a popular figure. Fans belt out his name during basketball games when they spot him watching from the northeast corner of the O'Connell Center.

getting ready to come over there and shake your hand." He would be the next coach at Florida.

At his press conference days later, Meyer talked about being a fan of Florida football during the 1990s. "At the University of Florida, you have everything in place to make a run at the whole thing, and that was a factor," he said. "I also recruited Florida for five years, and I understand the type of talent that you're playing with."

The task at hand was to get players who had been recruited by Ron Zook to buy into what Meyer was selling. But first, he had to coach his Utah team in the Fiesta Bowl. The Utes won 35–7 over Pittsburgh, and Meyer began to go to work full time at Florida. His contract: $14 million for seven years.

Master Motivator

Florida's players didn't have to wait long to see that things would be different under Urban Meyer. During summer workouts prior to his first season in 2005, Meyer banned the team from the locker room and told them they couldn't wear Gator gear. They would have to earn it.

Having been a psychology major in college at the University of Cincinnati, Meyer has used all forms of incentives to get his players' attention. He formed the Champions Club, where players who did what they were supposed to do would eat the best food. Those who didn't would get hot dogs. He made the players bond with their coaches, pushing them to have dinners at the homes of the assistants.

"They need to know that when they don't do the things they are supposed to do they are affecting families," he said.

Perhaps his best motivation ploy came the week before the 2006 BCS National Championship Game against Ohio State. Meyer had his staff put clippings of newspaper articles on a large board and placed it where the Gators would eat their team meals. In those articles were comments about how the Gators had no chance against the Buckeyes. It worked: Florida won 41–14.

Urban Meyer is one of those coaches who wears his emotions on his sleeve. He's not afraid to berate an official, fire up his team, and celebrate big plays with wild, animated gestures on the sidelines, as he does here during the 2005 Outback Bowl against Michigan.

Decorating this Gator pin is a montage of Chris Leak, who came to Florida as one of the biggest recruits ever. Despite some struggles along the way, Leak's legacy was that of a champion.

Excellent game coach led Florida to the 2006 National Title capped by the 41-14 pasting of Ohio State

A playing card depicts Urban Meyer, the Gator coach who now has two UF national titles under his belt. Meyer became a national figure when the Gators beat Ohio State 41–14 to win the 2006 national title.

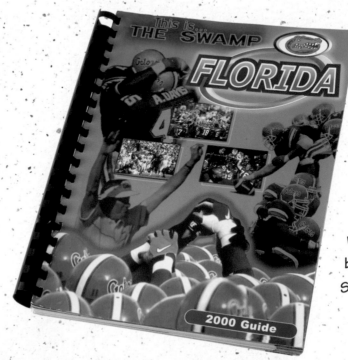

The 2000 media guide for Florida football was full of optimism despite the fact that the Gators hadn't won an SEC title since 1996. These Gators were not to be denied, beating Auburn to win the SEC title game.

The 2006 national title was part of an amazing run, when UF won two basketball and one football crown. Gainesville became known as "Titlesville."

Florida celebrated 100 years of football in 2006 with all kinds of memorabilia and on-the-field ceremonies. It turned out to be the celebration that wouldn't end, as Florida won the national title that season.

The media guide signaling Ron Zook's second season turned out to be an unexpected issue when the animal pictured on the cover was erroneously a crocodile instead of an alligator. Only at Florida could a detail like that get national exposure.

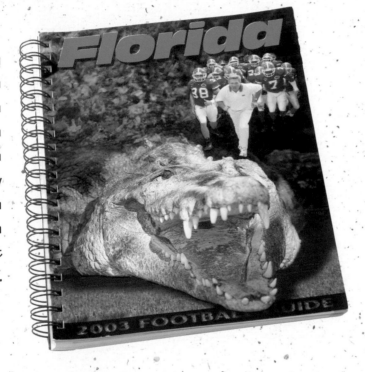

A ticket for the lower level at the Chick-fil-A Peach Bowl went for $70 in 2004. For that, Gator fans got to see their team lose 27–10 to Miami. Florida played the game with Charlie Strong serving as interim coach.

This poster celebrating Florida's 2006 national title includes the university's Century Tower in the upper right corner and the Gator Walk lined by palm trees.

The Urban Renewal

Florida's tradition of losing a midseason game to a team from the SEC West continued in 2007 with a 20–17 loss to Auburn. Florida trailed 14–0 at the half before Tim Tebow (15) rallied the Gators with a scoring pass and a touchdown run.

Urban Meyer had a major goal when he took over at Florida: Take back The Swamp.

Under Ron Zook, Florida had lost its home-field advantage, considered one of the best in football under Steve Spurrier. Under Spurrier, Florida had lost only five games at home in the span of 12 years. Under Zook, they lost six in three years.

"We've made a big deal about, 'That's our stadium. That's a sacred place,' " Meyer said in a press conference before his first SEC game in 2005. "That's a place that at one point the Gators didn't lose very often. We've discussed it at great length."

Meyer's Gators won that first SEC game in an intense battle with fifth-ranked Tennessee 16–7. And throughout the first season under Meyer, Florida did take back The Swamp, going 6–0 and beating FSU 34–7 to finish out the regular season.

The road was another story. Florida was handled by Alabama 31–3 in Tuscaloosa. After a difficult 21–17 loss two weeks later to LSU in Baton Rouge, Meyer was moved to tears in his postgame press conference. He had just left a locker room of crying players. For the first time, he believed his team was understanding what it took to be a winner.

More than anything, Meyer understood that his offense needed an adjustment. He inserted a fullback and tight end to certain formations in the spread offense and came away with a 14–10 win over Georgia.

With a shot at the SEC East on the line in Columbia against new Gamecocks coach Steve Spurrier, the Gators faltered again. They lost 30–22, and when the team returned to Gainesville, Meyer kept them in the plane for an emotional 30-minute speech.

It seemed to pay off with the win over FSU and an Outback Bowl victory over Iowa, which broke a three-game bowl losing streak for UF. Maybe the players were finally buying in. Maybe something wonderful was about to happen.

Florida defensive back Vernell Brown was called by Urban Meyer "the face of Florida football" during the 2005 season. Brown suffered a broken leg late in the season but returned in time for Florida's bowl game.

Oh My, It's Mick

He didn't think he had a chance. Mick Hubert, sports director at WHIO in Dayton, Ohio, sent the tape anyway back in 1989. Florida was looking for a new radio play-by-play man. "I remember thinking, 'They aren't going to hire me,'" he said. "I didn't have any connection to the University of Florida."

But they did. And he's grateful to have witnessed what he has seen over the last two decades. "I knew this was what I wanted to do," he said. "And I have been blessed."

If there are two things Florida fans have been able to count on during that span, it has been winning championships and Mick Hubert. During that time, he was working with different analysts in the booth. Former Gator player and coach Lee McGriff was on board at the beginning.

For two decades, Florida fans have been enjoying the play-by-play action brought to them by radio's Mick Hubert.

MICK HUBERT
Voice of the Gators
Ext. 6660
E-mail: mickh@gators.uaa.ufl.edu

UNIVERSITY ATHLETIC ASSOCIATION, INC.
UNIVERSITY OF FLORIDA
P.O. Box 14485, Gainesville, Florida 32604-2485

Florida WATS 1-800-34GATOR (4-2867)
(352) 375-GoUF (-4683)   FAX (352) 375-4803

Mick Hubert's signed business card probably should include an "Oh my!"—his trademark phrase after the Gators do something special on the field. Hubert has been the radio voice of the Gators throughout the best years of Florida football.

When McGriff's son Travis began playing for the Gators, he stepped aside. James Jones, a Gator great, took over. He left after three years, and former Gator linebacker Scot Brantley moved in.

When McGriff's children were all finished playing sports, he came back on board in 2004. "They were all great to work with," Hubert said. "The thing that is great about Lee is that he played and coached. I see the game like checkers, one move at a time. He sees it like chess, always thinking one move ahead."

Hubert borrowed Dick Enberg's expression to accentuate his broadcasts, shouting "Oh my!" after big plays. He began saying it in 1976 after a friend in Los Angeles sent him tapes of Enberg, a TV play-by-play man for NBC.

"Steve Spurrier was at a function one year and talked to Dick Enberg," Hubert said. "He told Steve, 'Tell your guy back there I stole it from someone in the 1940s.'"

"I knew this was what I wanted to do. And I have been blessed."

Mick Hubert

Glendale Glory

The 2006 football season for Florida was supposed to be about the past. It ended up being about the present.

In the 100th year of Florida football, there were ceremonies involving almost every game. The Ring of Honor was introduced, the 1996 team was honored, and there was a gala the night before the Alabama game. Florida even wore throwback uniforms for the game against the Crimson Tide. But all of the celebrations took a back seat to what was happening on the field.

In a year of tight games and big plays, Florida found itself in Glendale, Arizona, playing Ohio State for a national title. How the Gators got there was as much a part of the story as how they won it.

The Gators went to Knoxville, Tennessee, on September 16, 2006, where they trailed the Volunteers late in the game. There, Tebow-mania began. Quarterback Tim Tebow picked up a crucial fourth-and-one as the Gators drove for the winning score. The 21–20 victory was sealed thanks to an interception by safety Reggie Nelson.

Two big home wins over Alabama (28–13) and LSU (23–10) were closer than the scores indicated. The Gators needed big defensive plays by Nelson in each of them. By then, the pattern had been set. Florida was going to win with defense.

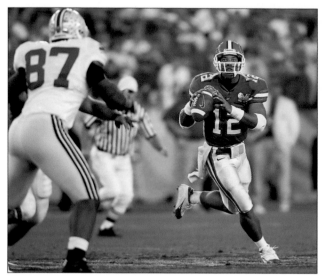

They were also going to win with a combination of Ron Zook's players and Urban Meyer's second recruiting class. Of the 22 starters, 21 of them were recruited by Zook. But true freshmen like Tebow and wide receiver Percy Harvin would play key roles.

The one loss came at Auburn, 27–17, when the Tigers won despite not scoring an offensive touchdown. In the locker room, players were angry. Fingers were pointed. Names were called out.

"It was wild," Meyer recalled later. "It was a tough deal. One of the coaches said, 'We've got to get this thing under

Tim Tebow (15), running for yardage against Tennessee, was a situational quarterback as a freshman in 2006. His short yardage runs were punctuated with precision passes. He accounted for 13 touchdowns as a freshman.

control,' and I said, 'No, let it go.' So we let it go for about 15 minutes. I wanted them to clear the air."

It seemed to work. UF finished off the regular season with five straight wins. But there were some tense moments. None were more tense than the South Carolina game on November 11.

The Gamecocks had a chance to end Florida's dream with a last-second field goal. Instead, defensive end Jarvis Moss jumped high in the air to block it and preserve the 17–16 score to win the game.

When Florida beat Arkansas 38–28 behind MVP Harvin, it was off to the desert to face Ohio State. There, the Gators dominated. After giving up a kickoff return touchdown to the Buckeyes' Ted Ginn Jr. on the first play, they outscored Ohio State 41–7. Ends Derrick Harvey and Moss pressured OSU quarterback Troy Smith into turnovers. Chris Leak was masterful in managing the offense, throwing the ball toward the roof of the domed stadium after the horn sounded.

"My legacy was to get the University of Florida back here," Leak said after the confetti had dropped.

Double Teamed

The Florida football team went directly from the airport to the O'Connell Center after winning the Bowl Championship Series national title game in Arizona. There, the football team would be honored at halftime.

As they were being cheered on the court, the Gator basketball team came back out to warm up. Joakim Noah, one of the hoops heroes, bear-hugged Florida linebacker Brandon Siler. Siler said to Noah, "It's back on you."

Already, Florida's hoopsters had won a national title in April by beating UCLA. When the football team won its crown, it was the first time in NCAA history that a school held both national championships.

But it wasn't over. The basketball team repeated in 2007 after a title win by the football team. Once again, Florida beat Ohio State with everything on the line.

They called Gainesville "Title-town" after the football team won a national championship that was sandwiched by a pair of men's basketball national crowns. Joakim Noah helped UF become the first school to own both the football and basketball titles at the same time.

Timmy Terrific

No sophomore had ever won the Heisman Trophy before Tim Tebow did it in 2007. He came close to becoming the second player to repeat when he finished third in 2008, despite receiving the most first-place votes.

Sitting on a plane heading to visit a recruit, Urban Meyer was nervous about Tim Tebow. The quarterback from Nease High School near St. Augustine, Florida, had been a Gator fan his whole life but was toying with the idea of going to Alabama.

"If we don't get him," said codefensive coordinator Greg Mattison, "it's going to set the program back ten years." Meyer looked at Mattison like he was crazy. "Ten years," Mattison repeated.

Fortunately, Florida fans never had to find out. Tebow committed and signed with Florida, and a legend was born.

It started with his freshman season when he bullied defenders on running plays and brought the jump pass back to the game. Already, the Tim Tebow jokes were making the rounds, most of them takeoffs on Chuck Norrisisms:

When the bogeyman goes to sleep every night, he checks the closet for Tim Tebow.

The active ingredient in Red Bull is Tim Tebow's sweat.

"The one I liked best was, 'Tim Tebow *can* believe it's not butter,'" Tebow said.

If Superman does indeed wear Tim Tebow pajamas, he wears them proudly. In 2007, Tebow took over the reins from Chris Leak and had a year like no player before him. He accounted for 55 touchdowns passing and rushing, breaking the SEC record for rushing touchdowns in a season and the NCAA record for touchdowns for a quarterback. For his efforts, in 2007 Tebow became the first sophomore to win the Heisman Trophy, college football's top award.

After receiving a hug from former Heisman winner Danny Wuerffel, Tebow gave a speech in which he said, "I love being a Gator" three times, eliciting chuckles from the crowd. "When I get back to the University of Florida, we're going to have fun."

He did the following year. Even though his numbers weren't as gaudy as the year before, Tebow guided the Gators to the national title game.

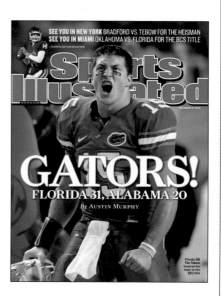

He had done so much as a quarterback, but there was one thing Tim Tebow hadn't done until Florida's SEC Championship Game victory over Alabama: He led the team from behind for the first time, pushing across to two fourth-quarter scores in the 31–20 win.

He was a Heisman finalist but finished third despite having the most first-place votes of any of the finalists.

A Crazy Year

The Heisman Trophy winner was back. So were most of the wide receivers and offensive linemen. But for Florida to repeat as national champions in 2007, a young defense would have to grow old in a hurry.

It didn't.

As a result, the Gators were on the cusp of greatness in 2007 but couldn't get over the hump. They were close, however.

Despite trailing 14–0 against Auburn at home, Tim Tebow rallied the Gators to tie the game at 17 in the second half, only to see Auburn march down the field for the game-winning field goal. The following week, Florida couldn't hold on to a 17–7 lead against No. 1 LSU and lost 28–24 as the Tigers converted five fourth-down attempts. A tearful Tebow left the field knowing that a return to the national title game was up in smoke.

Florida's defense was exposed by a fired-up Michigan team, playing in the last game coached by Lloyd Carr. The Wolverines won 41–35 despite three touchdown passes and a scoring run by quarterback Tim Tebow (15).

"Everyone played their hearts out; it just didn't fall correctly," said freshman cornerback Joe Haden. "No one could have played any harder than we did."

Then came the bizarre.

Florida still had a chance to win the SEC East but needed to beat rival Georgia. Tebow was suffering from a left shoulder contusion that limited his running. Georgia, which had lost two straight to UF and 15 of the last 17 to the Gators, needed a spark.

When Georgia running back Knowshon Moreno scored the first

touchdown of the game, the entire Georgia team stormed the field. Whether it inspired the Bulldogs more than the Gators is anyone's guess, but Georgia prevailed 42–30.

The hopes for the Eastern Division were gone, but Florida did win its next four games, including a 45–12 thumping of Florida State, to earn a berth opposite the University of Michigan in the Capital One Bowl.

But the defensive liabilities showed up against the Wolverines, who were playing their last game for outgoing coach Lloyd Carr. Michigan won 41–35, and Florida coach Urban Meyer vowed after the game to have a better defense in 2008.

It was a wild year for Florida, but one thing that was normal was a win over Florida State. Here, wide receiver Percy Harvin heads for a touchdown to help the Gators win their fourth straight over the Seminoles.

Gator Bytes

The Internet is certainly useful for football fans, but not always a bonus for the coaches. As soon as Ron Zook was hired by UF, a FireRonZook.com site was up and running and message boards started chirping.

It used to be that the only way to follow the Gators was through the newspaper, by listening to the radio, or watching TV for the highlights. But all that changed with the Internet.

Fan sites began to spring up like wildfire. The Web site GatorCountry.com made inroads in the 1990s and became an important bookmark for all Gator fans. Gatorbait.net, Gatorenvy.com, and Alligatorarmy.com also began to fill cyberspace with fan input. Popular chat boards on these sites gave fans an opportunity to vent as well as a place to spread rumors that sent journalists scurrying to check them out.

The newspapers themselves were slow to react to the Internet phenomenon but eventually jumped on board, giving the Gator Nation a multitude of sites to survey. Since six different state papers have reporters embedded in Gainesville, there is no shortage of blogs to read.

Internet sites such as Rivals and Scout have sections devoted to Florida football as well. And the University of Florida Athletic Association launched GatorZone.com as the official site of the Florida Gators, covering football as well as UF's many other women and men's sports teams.

The Internet also brought about a new phenomenon when a fan launched FireRonZook.com after Zook was hired as the Gator coach. It was infectious, with many fan bases starting their own Web sites that were critical of their coaches.

With the newspaper industry struggling during tough economic times, more emphasis has been put into their Web sites. For example, Gatorsports.com, the site belonging to *The Gainesville Sun*, has used blogs, Swampcasts (five-minute videos previewing and reviewing games), interactive trivia contests, chats, and previews of all the college football bowl games to keep its readers informed.

As the official Web site of the Florida Gators, GatorZone.com provides fans with everything from ticket information to a Fan Central section for posters, autograph requests, and more.

Triple Crown

After hearing for weeks how Oklahoma's offense could not be stopped, linebacker Brandon Spikes and the Florida defense had an answer. The Gators limited the Sooners to 14 points in the BCS National Championship Game.

Just before the Florida football team headed for a bus that would take them to Dolphin Stadium and the BCS National Championship Game, Gator coach Urban Meyer told his team that being in Miami was no fluke.

"This isn't good fortune the way you guys are playing, how the stars aligned right," Meyer said. "You might not get a chance to play with guys like this again. Make it count."

And they did. Florida's defense limited Oklahoma's offense—the highest scoring in college football history—to two touchdowns and came away with a 24–14 win and the Gators' third national title.

The win capped a remarkable 2008 season that seemed to be derailed in the fourth game of the season with a 31–30 home loss to Mississippi. But after that, the Gators went on an amazing roll. Over the next eight games they outscored the opposition 414–97 to set up a showdown with No. 1 Alabama for the SEC Championship.

In Atlanta, UF trailed 20–17 heading into the fourth quarter. But quarterback Tim Tebow led the Gators to a pair of scoring drives and a 31–20 victory. Florida outgained Alabama 134–1 in the fourth quarter.

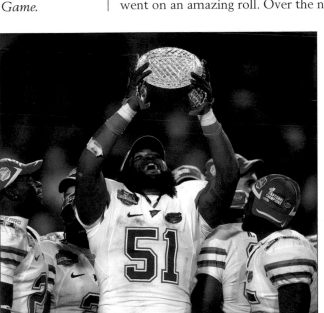

Promise Kept

The Ole Miss game had been over for about an hour when Tim Tebow came into the press conference. He had trouble composing himself before delivering a speech that would become the signature moment for the 2008 Gators, Later, Tebow would say he spent extra time at his locker after the game deciding what he would say.

"To the fans and everybody in Gator Nation, I'm sorry. Extremely sorry. We were hoping for an undefeated season, that was my goal, something Florida has never done here. I promise you one thing, a lot of good will come out of this.

"You have never seen any player in the entire country play as hard as I will play the rest of the season. You will never see someone push the rest of the team as hard as I will push everybody the rest of the season. You will never see a team play harder than we will the rest of the season. God bless."

And then he delivered.

After a heartbreaking loss to Ole Miss in the fourth game of the 2008 season, Tim Tebow gave an emotional speech after the game. Then, he and his teammates delivered with another national title.

"A lot was made of this game being the old versus the new, and yes, we've got speed," Meyer said. "But from Day One our program has been based on toughness."

It showed up again in Miami. Two goal-line stands and a pair of Tebow touchdown passes gave Florida the win. Three days later, Tebow announced he would return for his senior season during the Gators' national title celebration.

FLORIDA MEMORIES

The Gator logo is now recognized nationally, but it is relatively young, coming into play in the mid-1990s when UF commissioned a firm to update it.

This football celebrates the 2006 championship and includes the BCS logo. Add a signature by Urban Meyer or any of the Gator players who won the title, and you're looking at a valuable piece of memorabilia.

What would Christmas be without a Gator on the tree? Ornaments of all kinds are purchased by the Gator Nation each year.

For Florida fans, there are so many options for Game Day. For example, this faux jersey sporting the number 1 is one of many shirts that occupy the closets of Gator fans.

The alliteration makes "Go Gators" a memorable cheer, and this pin brings the cheer to the lips of every Florida fan. The "Gators" script on the helmet was a product of the Charley Pell regime and has lasted to today.

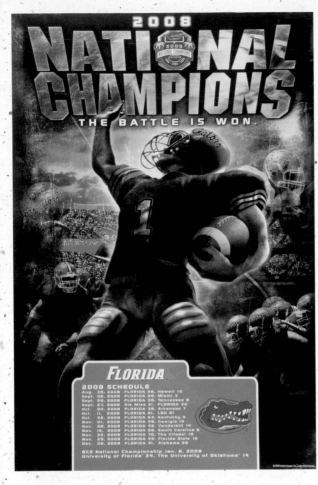

The 2008 national champion Gators are saluted on this poster, and what a season it was. The heartbreak of the Ole Miss loss was offset by an amazing run of points and victories, culminating in the 24–14 win over Oklahoma.

Some fans prefer a simple hat to show their support, while others go for bust, like the owner of this LED-lit cap.

The new front door of UF's stadium is the Gateway of Champions, honored here on this cereal box. Also pictured are three Gator legends—Chris Leak, Danny Wuerffel, and Jack Youngblood.

Earl Everett is Mr. July on this 2008 calendar. There aren't enough months in the year to salute all of the greatest Gators, but Everett became legendary when he made a tackle in the national title win over Ohio State despite losing his helmet.

FLORIDA BY THE NUMBERS

Annual Records 1906–2008

Year	Overall Record W	L	T	Conference Record W	L	T	F
1906	5	3	0	—	—	—	—
1907	4	1	1	—	—	—	—
1908	5	2	1	—	—	—	—
1909	6	1	1	—	—	—	—
1910	6	1	0	—	—	—	—
1911	5	0	1	—	—	—	—
1912	5	2	1	—	—	—	—
1913	4	3	0	—	—	—	—
1914	5	2	0	—	—	—	—
1915	4	3	0	—	—	—	—
1916	0	5	0	—	—	—	—
1917	2	4	0	—	—	—	—
1918	0	1	0	—	—	—	—
1919	5	3	0	—	—	—	—
1920	6	3	0	—	—	—	—
1921	6	3	2	—	—	—	—
1922	7	2	0	—	—	—	—
1923	6	1	2	—	—	—	—
1924	6	2	2	—	—	—	—
1925	8	2	0	—	—	—	—
1926	2	6	2	—	—	—	—
1927	7	3	0	—	—	—	—
1928	8	1	0	—	—	—	—

Year	Overall Record W	L	T	Conference Record W	L	T	F
1929	8	2	0	—	—	—	—
1930	6	3	1	—	—	—	—
1931	2	6	2	—	—	—	—
1932	3	6	0	—	—	—	—
1933	5	3	1	2	3	0	7th–T
1934	6	3	1	2	2	1	6th
1935	3	7	0	1	6	0	10th
1936	4	6	0	1	5	0	10th
1937	4	7	0	3	4	0	8th
1938	4	6	1	2	2	1	6th
1939	5	5	1	0	3	1	8th
1940	5	5	0	2	3	0	8th
1941	4	6	0	1	3	0	10th
1942	3	7	0	1	3	0	8th
1943	No Team			—	—	—	—
1944	4	3	0	0	3	0	9th
1945	4	5	1	1	3	1	8th–T
1946	0	9	0	0	5	0	11th
1947	4	5	1	0	3	1	9th
1948	5	5	0	1	5	0	9th–T
1949	4	5	1	1	4	1	10th–T
1950	5	5	0	2	4	0	8th
1951	5	5	0	2	4	0	6th–T
1952	8	3	0	3	3	0	6th

Year	Overall Record			Conference Record			
	W	L	T	W	L	T	F
1953	3	5	2	1	3	2	6th
1954	5	5	0	5	2	0	3rd–T
1955	4	6	0	3	5	0	8th
1956	6	3	1	5	2	0	3rd
1957	6	2	1	4	2	1	3rd–T
1958	6	4	1	2	3	1	7th–T
1959	5	4	1	2	4	0	7th
1960	9	2	0	5	1	0	2nd
1961	4	5	1	3	3	0	5th
1962	7	4	0	4	2	0	5th
1963	6	3	1	3	3	1	7th
1964	7	3	0	4	2	0	2nd–T
1965	7	4	0	4	2	0	3rd
1966	9	2	0	5	1	0	2nd
1967	6	4	0	4	2	0	3rd–T
1968	6	3	1	3	2	1	4th–T
1969	9	1	1	3	1	1	4th
1970	7	4	0	3	3	0	5th
1971	4	7	0	1	6	0	6th–T
1972	5	5	1	3	3	1	6th
1973	7	5	0	3	4	0	5th–T
1974	8	4	0	3	3	0	3rd–T
1975	9	3	0	5	1	0	2nd–T
1976	8	4	0	4	2	0	3rd
1977	6	4	1	3	3	0	5th
1978	4	7	0	3	3	0	4th–T
1979	0	10	1	0	6	0	9th–T
1980	8	4	0	4	2	0	3rd–T
1981	7	5	0	3	3	0	3rd–T
1982	8	4	0	3	3	0	5th–T
1983	9	2	1	4	2	0	3rd–T
1984	9	1	1	5	0	1	1st**
1985	9	1	1	5	1	0	1st–T***

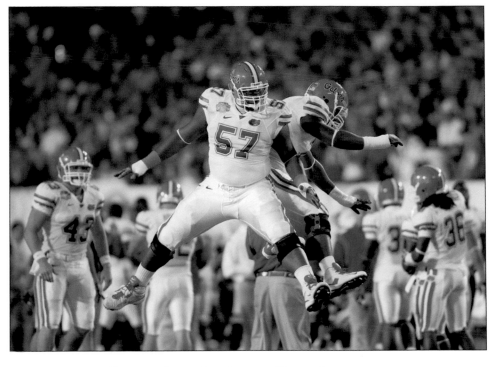

Year	Overall Record			Conference Record			
	W	L	T	W	L	T	F
1986	6	5	0	2	4	0	4th–T
1987	6	6	0	3	3	0	5th
1988	7	5	0	4	3	0	3rd–T
1989	7	5	0	4	3	0	2nd–T
1990	9	2	0	6	1	0	1st***
1991	10	2	0	7	0	0	1st*
1992	9	4	0	6	2	0	1st–T–East
1993	11	2	0	7	1	0	1st–East*
1994	10	2	1	7	1	0	1st–East*
1995	12	1	0	8	0	0	1st–East*
1996	12	1	0	8	0	0	1st–East*†
1997	10	2	0	6	2	0	3rd–T–East
1998	10	2	0	7	1	0	2nd–East
1999	9	4	0	7	1	0	1st–East
2000	10	3	0	7	1	0	1st–East*
2001	10	2	0	6	2	0	2nd–East

The 2008 Gators finished with a 13–1–0 record and won the BCS national championship.

Year	Overall Record			Conference Record			
	W	L	T	W	L	T	F
2002	8	5	0	6	2	0	2nd–East
2003	8	5	0	6	2	0	1st–T–East
2004	7	5	0	4	4	0	3rd–T–East
2005	9	3	0	5	3	0	2nd–T–East
2006	13	1	0	7	1	0	1st–East*†
2007	9	4	0	5	3	0	3rd–East
2008	13	1	0	7	1	0	1st–East*†

* Won SEC title

** SEC title vacated

*** Ineligible for SEC title

† Won national championship

Coaches

Coach	Years Overall	W–L–T	Winning Percentage
James A. Forsythe	1906–1908	14–6–2	.682
G. E. Pyle	1909–1913	26–7–3	.764
Charles McCoy	1914–1916	9–10–0	.474
A. L. Busser	1917–1919	7–8–0	.467
William Kline	1920–1922	19–8–2	.690
Gen. J. A. Van Fleet	1923–1924	12–3–4	.737
H. L. Sebring	1925–1927	17–11–2	.600
Charles Bachman	1928–1932	27–18–3	.594
D. K. Stanley	1933–1935	14–13–2	.517
Josh Cody	1936–1939	17–24–2	.419
Tom Lieb	1940–1942, 1944–1945	20–26–1	.436
Ray Wolf	1946–1949	13–24–2	.359
Bob Woodruff	1950–1959	53–42–6	.556
Ray Graves	1960–1969	70–31–4	.686
Doug Dickey	1970–1978	58–43–2	.573
Charley Pell	1979–1984	33–26–3	.549
Galen Hall	1984–1989	40–18–1	.686
Gary Darnell*	1989	3–4–0	.429

Coach	Years Overall	W–L–T	Winning Percentage
Steve Spurrier	1990–2001	122–27–1	.817
Ron Zook	2002–2004	23–14–0	.621
Charlie Strong*	2004	0–1–0	.000
Urban Meyer	2005–present	44–9–0	.830

* Interim coach

Bowl Games

Season	Bowl	Results
1952	Gator Bowl	Florida 14, Tulsa 13
1958	Gator Bowl	Ole Miss 7, Florida 3
1960	Gator Bowl	Florida 13, Baylor 12
1962	Gator Bowl	Florida 17, Penn State 7
1965	Sugar Bowl	Missouri 20, Florida 18
1966	Orange Bowl	Florida 27, Georgia Tech 12
1969	Gator Bowl	Florida 14, Tennessee 13
1973	Tangerine Bowl	Miami of Ohio 16, Florida 7
1974	Sugar Bowl	Nebraska 13, Florida 10
1975	Gator Bowl	Maryland 13, Florida 0

Current UF coach Urban Meyer owns the highest winning percentage in history among UF coaches.

Season	Bowl	Results
1976	Sun Bowl	Texas A&M 37, Florida 14
1980	Tangerine Bowl	Florida 35, Maryland 20
1981	Peach Bowl	West Virginia 26, Florida 6
1982	Bluebonnet Bowl	Arkansas 28, Florida 24
1983	Gator Bowl	Florida 14, Iowa 6
1987	Aloha Bowl	UCLA 20, Florida 16
1988	All-American Bowl	Florida 14, Illinois 10
1989	Freedom Bowl	Washington 34, Florida 7
1991	Sugar Bowl	Notre Dame 39, Florida 28
1992	Gator Bowl	Florida 27, NC State 10
1993	Sugar Bowl	Florida 41, West Virginia 7
1994	Sugar Bowl	Florida State 23, Florida 17
1995	Fiesta Bowl	Nebraska 62, Florida 24
1996	Sugar Bowl	Florida 52, Florida State 20
1997	Citrus Bowl	Florida 21, Penn State 6
1998	Orange Bowl	Florida 31, Syracuse 10
1999	Citrus Bowl	Michigan St. 37, Florida 34
2000	Sugar Bowl	Miami 37, Florida 20
2001	Orange Bowl	Florida 56, Maryland 23
2002	Outback Bowl	Michigan 38, Florida 30
2003	Outback Bowl	Iowa 37, Florida 17
2004	Peach Bowl	Miami 27, Florida 10
2005	Outback Bowl	Florida 31, Iowa 24
2006	BCS Championship	Florida 41, Ohio State 14
2007	Capital One Bowl	Michigan 41, Florida 35
2008	BCS Championship	Florida 24, Oklahoma 14

College Football Hall of Fame

Player	Position	Inducted
Dale Van Sickel	End	1975
Charles Bachman	Coach	1978
Steve Spurrier	Quarterback	1986
Ray Graves	Coach	1990
Jack Youngblood	Defensive End	1992

Player	Position	Inducted
Doug Dickey	Coach	2003
Emmitt Smith	Running Back	2006
Wilber Marshall	Linebacker	2008

Heisman Trophy Winners

Steve Spurrier (1966)

Danny Wuerffel (1996)

Tim Tebow (2007)

First-Team All-Americans

Year	Player	Position
1928	Dale Van Sickel	End
1941	Forrest "Fergie" Ferguson	End
1952	Charles LaPradd	Tackle
1956	John Barrow	Guard
1958	Vel Heckman	Tackle
1964	Larry Dupree	Fullback
1965	Bruce Bennett	Defensive Back
1965	Charles Casey	End
1965	Larry Gagner	Guard
1965	Lynn Matthews	Defensive End
1965	Steve Spurrier	Quarterback
1966	Bill Carr	Center
1966	Steve Spurrier	Quarterback
1968	Guy Dennis	Guard
1968	Larry Smith	Fullback
1969	Carlos Alvarez	Wide Receiver
1969	Steve Tannen	Defensive Back
1970	Jack Youngblood	Defensive End
1971	John Reaves	Quarterback
1974	Burton Lawless	Guard
1974	Ralph Ortega	Linebacker
1975	Sammy Green	Linebacker
1976	Wes Chandler	Wide Receiver

Year	Player	Position
1988	Trace Armstrong	Defensive Tackle
1989	Emmitt Smith	Running Back
1990	Huey Richardson	Defensive End
1990	Will White	Free Safety
1991	Brad Culpepper	Defensive Tackle
1993	Judd Davis	Kicker
1993	Errict Rhett	Running Back
1994	Jack Jackson	Wide Receiver
1994	Kevin Carter	Defensive End
1995	Jason Odom	Tackle
1995	Danny Wuerffel	Quarterback
1996	Reidel Anthony	Wide Receiver
1996	Danny Wuerffel	Quarterback
1996	Ike Hilliard	Wide Receiver
1997	Jacquez Green	Wide Receiver
1997	Fred Weary	Cornerback
1997	Fred Taylor	Running Back
1998	Jevon Kearse	Linebacker
1998	Mike Peterson	Linebacker
1999	Alex Brown	Defensive End
2000	Lito Sheppard	Defensive Back
2001	Alex Brown	Defensive End
2001	Jabar Gaffney	Wide Receiver
2001	Rex Grossman	Quarterback
2001	Mike Pearson	Tackle
2003	Keiwan Ratliff	Cornerback
2003	Shannon Snell	Guard
2006	Reggie Nelson	Safety
2007	Percy Harvin	Wide Receiver
2007	Tim Tebow	Quarterback
2008	Percy Harvin	Wide Receiver
2008	Brandon James	Kick Returner
2008	Brandon Spikes	Linebacker
2008	Tim Tebow	Quarterback

Wide receiver Reidel Anthony made First-Team All-American in 1996.

Year	Player	Position
1977	Wes Chandler	Wide Receiver
1980	David Little	Linebacker
1980	Cris Collinsworth	Wide Receiver
1981	David Galloway	Defensive Tackle
1982	Wilber Marshall	Linebacker
1983	Wilber Marshall	Linebacker
1984	Lomas Brown	Tackle
1984	Alonzo Johnson	Linebacker
1985	Alonzo Johnson	Linebacker
1985	Jeff Zimmerman	Guard
1986	Jeff Zimmerman	Guard
1987	Louis Oliver	Defensive Back
1987	Clifford Charlton	Linebacker
1987	Jarvis Williams	Defensive Back
1988	Louis Oliver	Free Safety

Stat Leaders

Rushing

Most Rushing Yards, Game: Emmitt Smith, 316 (vs. New Mexico, 1989)

Most Rushing Yards, Season: Emmitt Smith, 1,599 (1989)

Most Rushing Yards, Career: Errict Rhett, 4,163 (1990–93)

Most Touchdowns in a Game: Tim Tebow, 5 (vs. South Carolina, 2007)

Most Touchdowns, Season: Tim Tebow, 23 (2007)

Most Touchdowns, Career: Tim Tebow, 43 (2006–present)

Most 100-Yard Games, Career: Emmitt Smith, 23 (1987–89)

Quarterback Tim Tebow reigns over several stats, including most rushing touchdowns in a season (23).

Longest Run: Emmitt Smith, 96 yards (vs. Mississippi State in 1988)

Most Yards per Carry, Career: Tony Green, 5.8 in 445 attempts (1974–77)

Most Average Yards Rushing per Game, Career: Emmitt Smith, 126.7 (1987–89)

Passing

Most Passing Yards, Game: Rex Grossman, 464 (vs. LSU, 2001)

Most Passing Yards, Season: Rex Grossman, 3,896 (2001)

Most Passing Yards, Career: Chris Leak, 11,213 (2003–06)

Most Touchdown Passes, Game: Doug Johnson, 7 (vs. Central Michigan, 1997) and Terry Dean, 7 (vs. New Mexico State, 1994)

Most Touchdown Passes, Season: Danny Wuerffel, 39 (1996)

Most Touchdown Passes, Career: Danny Wuerffel, 114 (1993–96)

Most Completions, Game: Rex Grossman, 36 (vs. Georgia, 2002)

Most Completions, Season: Rex Grossman, 287 (2002)

Most Completions, Career: Chris Leak, 895 (2003–06)

Highest Completion Percentage, Career: Tim Tebow, 65.8%, 448 of 681 (2006–present)

Longest Touchdown Pass: Cris Collinsworth to Derrick Gaffney (99 yards vs. Rice, 1977)

Receiving

Most Receptions, Game: Carlos Alvarez, 15 (vs. Miami, 1969)

Most Receptions, Season: Carlos Alvarez, 88 (1969) and Chad Jackson, 88 (2005)

Most Receptions, Career: Andre Caldwell, 185 (2003–07)

Most Yards Receiving, Game: Taylor Jacobs, 246 (vs. UAB, 2002)

Most Yards Receiving, Season: Travis McGriff, 1,357 (1998)

Most Yards Receiving, Career: Carlos Alvarez, 2,563 (1969–71)

Most Touchdowns Receiving, Game: Ike Hilliard, 4 (vs. Tennessee, 1995) and Jack Jackson, 4 (vs. New Mexico State, 1994)

Most Touchdowns Receiving, Season: Reidel Anthony, 18 (1996)

Most Touchdowns Receiving, Career: Chris Doering, 31 (1992–95)

Most 100-Yard Games, Career: Jabar Gaffney, 14 (2000–01)

Most Yards per Reception, Career: Wes Chandler, 21.3 (1974–77)

Kicking

Most Total Points, Career: Jeff Chandler, 368 (67 field goals, 167 extra points; 1997–2001)

Best Punting Average, Career: Ray Criswell, 44.4 (1982–85)

Defense

Most Interceptions, Season: Keiwan Ratliff, 9 (2003)

Most Interceptions, Career: Fred Weary, 15 (1994–97)

Longest Interception Return: Jackie Simpson, 100 yards (vs. Mississippi State, 1955) and Joe Brodsky, 100 yards (vs. Mississippi State, 1956)

Most Tackles, Season: Sammy Green, 202 (1976)

Most Tackles, Career: David Little, 475 (1977–80)

Most Sacks, Season: Alex Brown, 13 (1999)

Most Sacks, Career: Alex Brown, 33 (1998–2001)

Most Tackles for a Loss, Season: Wilber Marshall, 27 (1981)

Most Tackles for a Loss, Career: Wilber Marshall, 58 (1980–83)

Most Passes Broken Up, Career: Anthone Lott, 42 (1993–96)

Most Forced Fumbles, Career: Clifford Charlton, 15 (1984–87)

Most Fumbles Recovered, Career: Brandon Siler, 8 (2004–06) and Todd Johnson, 8 (1998–2002)

INDEX

This is...
THE SWAMP